THE POTLUCK

COOKBOOK

CLASSIC RECIPES FOR ANY OCCASION

BY

DOLORES KOSTELNI

To Marty Campbell
Enjoy!
Dolores Kostelni
11/2005

COLLECTORS PRESS

PORTLAND, OREGON

Cover Design: Lisa M. Douglass, Collectors Press, Inc.
Designer: Kevin A. Welsch, Collectors Press, Inc.
Editorial Manager: Jennifer Weaver-Neist, Collectors Press, Inc.
Editor: Sue Mann   Proofreader: Jade Chan

Kostelni, Dolores.
  The potluck cookbook : classic recipes for any occasion / by Dolores Kostelni.-- 1st American ed.
     p.   cm.
Includes index.
ISBN 1-933112-14-X (hardcover : alk. paper)
  1. Cookery, American. I. Title.
TX715.K7485 2005
641.5973--dc22
                              2005012808
Printed in Singapore
9 8 7 6 5 4 3 2 1

DEDICATION

To Jim, my dear husband for these forty-five-plus years, who dined enthusiastically on my potluck dishes — even the flops.

To my children — JH, Charles and Maria, Jeff and Anna, Hugo and Judy, and Natalie and Dan — and their families: honestly, you've always made dinner a delicious experience.

ACKNOWLEDGEMENTS

To my official dessert tasters at BONTEX: thank you sweetly.

To Antonia Allegra, director of the Food Writers Symposium at the Greenbrier: I've learned mightily from your intense "graduate writing courses."

A special thanks to my relatives, friends, and colleagues, who rallied to *The Potluck Cookbook* concept by contributing tasty recipes.

I'm grateful to the brilliant, creative staff at Collectors Press, from CEO/publisher Richard Perry to editorial manager Jennifer Weaver-Neist, who kept me on track, to publicity pro Laura Bartroff, and to the entire staff, especially graphic designer Kevin A. Welsch, who helped to create this gorgeous cookbook.

Your **free enhanced version** of this book is at www.enhancedbooks.com! Visit today.

193☐311☐21☐4x

TABLE OF CONTENTS

INTRODUCTION

Mention the word *potluck* and eyes light up. Everyone loves a potluck party: It means an abundance of delicious food and lots of great conversation. It also means that a great amount of pleasure can come from a small amount of individual effort. Usually each guest brings just one dish, and even though there's no set menu, a variety of preparations — exotic, regional, and family favorites — crowd the table. Potlucks are the real banquet, a feast of great aromas, flavors, and delicious preparations.

Potluck is an American word defined as "the luck or chance of a meal." The dictionary describes *potluck dinner* as "covered dish meals," and Ralph Waldo Emerson used potluck to describe unplanned happenings, as in "the potluck of the day."

Potluck is always a surprise. In *The Potluck Cookbook: Classic Recipes for Any Occasion*, potluck means a meal to which guests contribute covered dishes, or casseroles, for everyone's dining pleasure. *The Potluck Cookbook* contains plenty of easily prepared, tasty, and portable recipes — many old-time classics with some newly embraced combinations as well as a few ethnic specialties — but all are well-put-together casseroles incorporating the layering and melding of quality ingredients.

Planned for holidays, milestones, sporting events, brunches, and casual get-togethers, potlucks combine guests' diverse culinary talents and tastes. That's how it happened at the first Thanksgiving celebration: Native Americans and Pilgrims brought their favorite dishes to the harvest feast. That dinner joined the two groups into a community and provided both with plenty of good food as well as fun and friendship. It established the practice of everyone contributing specialty dishes as well as setting aside a special day for giving thanks, two customs we continue today. Potlucks are indeed an American tradition.

During the early days of our country, when the colonies thrived, churches became the gathering places. Colonists got to know one another over potlucks. They discussed the politics of the day, the new teacher at the schoolhouse, and the weather. During wars churches provided places for nourishment for the body as well as for the soul. The tradition of meeting and feasting in churches continues to this day. When my children were growing up, they knew which ones were "the good eating churches."

Potlucks translate into an efficient, economical, and delicious way to throw a party, and *The Potluck Cookbook* furnishes the recipes and plans. It offers seven themed chapters with wide-ranging recipes for get-togethers and celebrations, whether casual or elegant: tailgate parties, breakfasts and brunches, late dinners after the concert, holiday dinners, soup parties, or Saturday night dance parties. Chapter eight makes potluck events and celebrations a little easier to plan by suggesting specific menus for special occasions.

Potluck fare is as individual as the people who attend. Even though guests may not discuss what they're bringing, somehow the meal turns out to be terrific, with a balance of dishes in every category. Potlucks are convenient, too. *The Potluck Cookbook* gives the hostess comfort in knowing everything will be ready on time and no one will become harried or frazzled. And many of the simplest but most exquisite recipes can be made before they're needed.

Potlucks accommodate any size group at any hour of the day. Even when a potluck party is small – eight for bridge on Saturday night, for example – the hostess may assign a different part of the meal to each couple. *The Potluck Cookbook* has just the right recipes for this situation, with superb party starters, entrées, vegetables and salads, and grand finales. Breakfast and brunch fit right in with the potluck concept, too, whether it's for a meet-the-candidate political gathering or a neighborhood get-together.

When I moved to the Shenandoah Valley of Virginia as a bride, potlucks became paramount to my social life. Church suppers, bridge club lunches, garden club teas, wedding receptions, informal affairs held in church basements or outdoors in pretty backyards all

inspired guests to bring their best. People ate heartily after attending funerals, too; early on I learned that these get-togethers required wholesome foods.

Events bring family and friends together to break bread, to enjoy great fellowship with on-the-spot conversations about covered-dish recipes. Potlucks create an energy all their own and provide the impetus for meeting people and for networking while having a fabulous time. All the recipes in *The Potluck Cookbook* call for ingredients easily found in any supermarket. The recipes come together easily, and they're practical, beautiful, delicious, and portable. There's potluck a-plenty for everyone.

A LITTLE HISTORY: THE DISH ON POTLUCKS AND CASSEROLES

The word potluck is American, but casserole derives from the Greek *kyathion*, the Latin *cattia*, and the Old French *casse*. Because a casserole is a container in which food is baked and served, potlucks and casseroles go hand in hand.

Historians give credit to the ancient Greeks for putting the concept of potluck meals into action. The Greeks brought their slowly cooked casseroles to a central location after planting and harvesting were done. Those dishes, using combinations of vegetables, grains, meats, potatoes, beans, and rice, enhanced workers' revelry and relaxation after weeks of hard work. Sharing food and having a good time were the main purposes, and casseroles made small amounts of food go far. Cooks, servants, field hands, housekeepers

— everyone brought dishes to the table, the food combinations and tastes depending on availability, personal preferences, and the time of year and day the meal was held. Delicious dishes and social dimensions were important facets of Greek culture, which reflected on their high standard of living and their pleasures derived from enjoying fine food in good company.

Potluck parties in America go back to the first Thanksgiving at Plymouth Colony. They were popular during colonial days, too, but with the introduction of canned soups in the early twentieth century, the Campbell Soup Company made casserole — and therefore potluck — history. Campbell's advertisements trumpeted how a can or two of soup effortlessly transforms complex French dishes and sauces into easily put-together, delectable meals busy American homemakers desired.

When Clarence Birdseye began freezing foods in 1924, his innovative products also helped homemakers. Packaged frozen vegetables were handy for use anytime — and when thawed, they looked and tasted like the fresh ones. The homemaker's meal planning now depended on her pantry and freezer inventory; consequently, cooking took mere minutes instead of many hours. Potluck dinners became easier than ever.

Neighborhood or block potluck parties emerged as a major social trend during World War II. Many women worked in defense plants; little time remained for them to socialize except at neighborhood potluck get-togethers. As couples moved to suburbia after the war, potluck parties maintained their star status. The suburban homemaker baked her dishes in gorgeous two-piece casseroles that took their rightful place on the table whether for company or for the family.

Potluck dishes offer every cook endless opportunities to define a personal culinary style. Whether homey or sophisticated, well-constructed casseroles are the highlight of potluck buffet parties, family reunions, holidays, and celebrations. Even though we use ovens to bake our casseroles, the basic plan of combining a few or several ingredients to make a meal in a pot (or a casserole) endures.

PARTY-STARTERS, SLOW COOKER SOUPS, AND APPETIZER CASSEROLES

Jump-start the conviviality at your next potluck party with a tried-and-true casserole, quiche, or molded salmon pâté. Guests will enjoy these fuss-free preparations, and with everyone sharing in the cooking, you'll be the cool host by spending quality time with your guests. Or try a potluck soup party. It's one of the best parties ever, showing off a parade of slow cookers burbling with several delicious soups.

HOT ARTICHOKE AND SPINACH DIP IN A BREAD CASSEROLE

This great dip bakes in its own edible casserole. Its presentation has a way of breaking the ice in a hurry if you're a newcomer at a potluck party. Note that the bread must dry overnight before using.

> 1 loaf unsliced round rye bread or other unsliced round loaf
>
> 2 6-ounce jars marinated artichoke hearts, well drained and chopped
>
> 1 10-ounce package frozen, chopped spinach, thawed and squeezed of liquid
>
> 1 1/2 cups mayonnaise
>
> 1 clove garlic, minced
>
> 1/3 cup chopped fresh parsley
>
> 1 1/2 cups grated Parmesan cheese

1. Hollow out the bread using a sharp, long-bladed knife, leaving a 1 1/2- to 2-inch rim around the edges. Cube the bread taken from the center and transfer to a plastic bag. Dry the hollowed loaf overnight at room temperature.

2. Preheat the oven to 275°F.

3. Place the artichoke hearts with the spinach, mayonnaise, garlic, parsley, and Parmesan cheese in the workbowl of a food processor and pulse to coarsely chop and combine. Transfer the mixture to the hollowed loaf. Wrap the loaf loosely in heavy-duty foil and place on a baking sheet.

4. Bake 2 1/2 hours. Transfer to a serving tray or napkin-lined large, shallow basket by sliding two spatulas underneath the loaf at opposite sides. Turn down the foil to partially unwrap the loaf. Surround the loaf with reserved bread chunks, crackers, and cucumber rounds.

SERVES AT LEAST 8

TIP: For a Mexican flavor, add 3 tablespoons of well-drained salsa.

11

A-CUP-A-CUP-A-CUP DIP

You would be amazed at the number of times this dip with the silly name has come to the rescue. It's a tasty something to whip up and serve to unexpected guests or to bring to a potluck party.

1 cup mayonnaise
1 cup sour cream
1 cup chopped green pepper
1 tablespoon instant minced onion
1 tablespoon dried parsley flakes
1 teaspoon dried dill

1. Combine all the ingredients by hand and place in a 3- or 4-cup bowl suitable for serving. If possible, cover with plastic wrap and refrigerate at least 4 hours for the flavors to blend or serve immediately.

2. Place in the center of a tray and surround with sturdy chips, crackers, and vegetables for dipping.

MAKES ABOUT 3 CUPS

TIP: Add chopped black olives or a spoonful of various tapenades, chutneys, jalepeño jelly, or a little picante sauce to make an excellent, well-seasoned dip.

PARTY SPINACH BALLS WITH HORSERADISH CURRY DIP

Ever popular and welcome at any get-together, this combination of spinach, eggs, stuffing and seasonings is fun to make and easy to eat. These are delicious hot and plain from the oven or dipped into well-seasoned hot or cold dips, such as a cheese fondue or a Horseradish Curry Dip.

2 boxes (10 ounces each) frozen chopped spinach, thawed, squeezed dry
2 cups herb stuffing
1 small onion, chopped
4 large eggs, beaten
3/4 cup (1 1/2 sticks) unsalted butter, melted
1/2 teaspoon garlic powder
1/2 cup grated Parmesan cheese

1. Lightly oil two baking sheets and set aside.

2. Mix the spinach with the stuffing, onion, eggs, butter, garlic powder, and cheese in a large bowl. Cover and refrigerate at least 2 hours to chill.

3. Preheat the oven to 350°F.

4. Shape the mixture into tablespoon-size balls and place on the prepared baking sheets.

5. Bake 20 minutes. Serve hot or warm with toothpicks and favorite dips.

MAKES AT LEAST 60 BALLS

HORSERADISH CURRY DIP

1 cup whole egg mayonnaise
1 tablespoon grated onion
1 teaspoon horseradish
1 teaspoon curry powder
1/2 to 1 teaspoon garlic salt
1/2 to 1 teaspoon white wine vinegar

1. Mix all the ingredients together in a medium bowl. Cover and refrigerate 12 to 24 hours.

2. Transfer the mixture to an attractive bowl placed in the middle of a tray. Surround it with Party Spinach Balls.

MAKES 1 CUP

CITRUS-MARINATED SHRIMP

A pleasant and refreshing marinade lightly seasons cooked shrimp and makes them special. For the best flavor, marinate a few hours before serving.

1/3 cup olive oil

3 tablespoons fresh lemon juice

2 tablespoons fresh lime juice

3 tablespoons fresh orange juice

1 small clove garlic, finely minced (optional)

1/4 cup finely minced parsley leaves

3/4 teaspoon dried thyme leaves

3/4 teaspoon salt

1/4 teaspoon black pepper

1 1/2 pounds medium shrimp, cooked, shelled, and cleaned

1. Combine all the ingredients except the shrimp. Place the shrimp in a medium bowl and pour the marinade over them. Mix with your hands or two wooden spoons to combine. Cover and refrigerate a few hours.

2. Drain the marinade and place the shrimp in a glass bowl or a dish lined with Boston lettuce leaves. Serve chilled with toothpicks.

SERVES 6 TO 8

TIP: If you prefer to omit the garlic, increase the thyme leaves to 1 teaspoon.

QUICHE LORRAINE

Julia Child introduced us to quiche in the 1950s on her cooking show, *The French Chef*. Julia suggested partially baking the pie shell because it gives a crisper crust.

1 9-inch ready-made piecrust, partially baked if desired

1/2 pound bacon, crisp, drained, and coarsely crumbled

3/4 cup shredded swiss cheese, divided

3 large eggs, blended

1 cup half-and-half or heavy cream

1/2 teaspoon salt

1/4 teaspoon white pepper

1. Preheat the oven to 375°F. Line the pie dish with the crust, turning the overhang under itself and fluting the edges. Bake 8 to 10 minutes or until golden; bake approximately 5 minutes if partially baking (see headnote).

2. Distribute the bacon over the shell. Spread 1/2 cup of cheese over the bacon.

3. Combine eggs with half-and-half, salt, and pepper. Pour the egg combination over the cheese. Sprinkle the remaining 1/4 cup of cheese over the top.

4. Bake 35 to 40 minutes or until golden brown and a knife inserted in the center comes out clean. Allow the quiche to settle 5 minutes before cutting. Serve hot or warm from the pie dish.

SERVES 6

TIP: Adapt this recipe to create different kinds of quiche. Add well-drained chopped spinach, canned tuna or salmon, cooked vegetables, or cooked and drained sausage.

MEXICAN ONION PIE

My longtime friend Jeanette Diver raved about this recipe so often I had to have it.

1 cup crumbled crackers, such as Ritz crackers

3 to 4 tablespoons melted butter

2 to 3 tablespoons butter

2 cups sweet onions, sliced into rings

1 cup shredded cheddar or swiss cheese, divided

2 large eggs, blended

1/2 cup milk or half-and-half

1 4-ounce can diced or chopped green chiles, drained

pinch salt

1/4 teaspoon black pepper, or to taste

1. Preheat the oven to 375°F. Lightly butter a 9-inch pie dish.

2. Combine the crackers with the melted butter. Reserve 1 tablespoon; distribute the remainder evenly over the bottom and sides of the pie dish to make a crust and set aside.

3. Melt the butter in a skillet, add the onions, and sauté over moderate heat until soft.

4. Spread 1/2 cup of cheese over the cracker crust. Place the onions over the cheese.

5. Combine the eggs with the milk, the remaining 1/2 cup of cheese, chiles, salt, and pepper. Pour over the onions, moving the onions with a fork to nudge the liquid down. Sprinkle the remaining 1 tablespoon cracker crumbs over the top.

6. Bake 35 to 45 minutes or until a knife inserted in several places comes out clean. Allow the pie to settle 5 minutes before cutting into pieces.

SERVES 6

TIP: Several varieties of sweet onions are on the market today. Consider USA-grown Walla Walla, Bermuda, and Vidalia onions or the South American OSO Sweet onions harvested at the foot of the Andes Mountains.

SALMON PÂTÉ

The combination of flavors makes this dish a favorite with everyone. Note that the pâté must be refrigerated at least 8 hours.

1 1-pound can salmon, well drained
2 4-ounce packages cream cheese with chives,
    cut into pieces
1 tablespoon dried minced onion
1 tablespoon lemon juice
1 tablespoon prepared horseradish
1 teaspoon snipped fresh chives
sliced black olives
sliced pimento-stuffed green olives
1/4 cup chopped fresh parsley leaves

1. Oil a 2-cup fish mold. Shape a piece of plastic wrap with a 3-inch overhang to fit the contours of the mold and set aside.

2. Place the salmon on a flat plate and remove all bones and skin. Place the salmon in the workbowl of a food processor fitted with the metal blade. Add the cream cheese, onion, lemon juice, horseradish, and chives. Pulse several times to combine the ingredients. Scrape the workbowl up from the bottom and along the sides. Process the mixture until it is well combined and smooth.

3. Transfer the mixture to the mold, smoothing the top with a small spatula. Bring the plastic wrap overhang to the center of the mold to cover the ingredients, adding more wrap if necessary. Refrigerate 8 hours or overnight.

4. Unfold the plastic wrap and place a serving dish over the salmon. Holding the dish and the mold together, turn both over so the dish is on the bottom. Remove the mold and carefully peel away the wrap.

5. Decorate the pâté according to your preference, such as placing a furled pimento strip encircled by a green olive slice for the eye. Arrange a thick bouquet of parsley sprigs at the tail and insert black olive slices for scales. Refrigerate, loosely covered, until needed. Serve with halved slices of cocktail rye or crackers.

SERVES 15

TIPS: Use a bowl with a narrow base if you don't have a fish mold. The pâté also makes an attractive log rolled in finely minced parsley for decoration.

SLOW COOKER CHILI CON QUESO

This is an emotional favorite because it was the first fondue I made. Little has changed; the flavors remain just as delicious today as they were years ago, but now I am more expansive with seasonings and dippers. Add more chiles and hot sauce if you prefer fire on your tongue.

1 pound processed cheese, such as Velveeta,
   cut into small cubes
1 cup shredded cheddar cheese
1 cup shredded Monterey Jack cheese
1 tablespoon cornstarch
2 tablespoons vegetable oil
4 scallions, chopped
1 14.5-ounce can stewed tomatoes, crushed
1 16-ounce can chili beans, drained (optional)
1 cup white wine
1 4-ounce can chopped or diced green chiles (optional)
dash or more of hot sauce (optional)
chopped cilantro

1. Oil the slow cooker pot. Toss the cheeses with the cornstarch and place in the cooker.

2. Warm the oil in a skillet and add the scallions. Cook over moderate heat until soft. Add the tomatoes and cook until most of the liquid evaporates. Add the beans, if using, and wine; bring to a boil.

3. Transfer the mixture into the cooker. Add the chiles, if using, and the hot sauce, if using. Stir to combine all the ingredients. Cover and cook on low about 3 hours, stirring from time to time.

4. Stir in the cilantro just before serving. Serve piping hot from the cooker, accompanied by big sturdy corn-chip dippers, wide pepper strips, broccoli and cauliflower florets, zucchini and yellow squash rounds, and pita triangles. Make sure you have plenty of dishes, napkins, and utensils on hand.

SERVES AT LEAST 8 TO 10

TIP: Make your *queso* different each time. Add sliced olives, more hot stuff, sliced scallions, or *salsa verde*.

QUICK AND EASY LAYERED MEXICAN DIP

This basic dip has the capacity to accommodate whichever add-ons or cutbacks you wish to make. It looks best on a large round platter to show off the layers and to make it easy for guests to scoop and dip. Note that the dip must be refrigerated several hours before serving.

1 16-ounce can refried beans

3 tablespoons salsa

1 tablespoon packaged taco seasoning mix

1 1/2 cups sour cream

1 cup prepared guacamole

1/4 cup chopped green bell pepper

4 scallions, trimmed, finely sliced, and divided

2 large ripe tomatoes, peeled, seeded, and chopped

1/2 cup sliced green olives with pimentos, drained, rinsed, and patted dry

1/2 cup sliced black olives, drained, rinsed, and patted dry

1 4-ounce can chopped or diced green chiles

1 1/4 cups shredded cheddar cheese

1/4 cup chopped cilantro

1. Combine the beans, salsa, and taco seasoning in a medium bowl. Spread the mixture on a large serving platter or tray. Spread the sour cream over the beans, leaving a 1-inch border of beans exposed. Spread the guacamole over the sour cream, leaving a border of sour cream exposed. Distribute the green pepper over the guacamole. Sprinkle half of the scallions over the peppers. Distribute the tomatoes over the onions, followed by the green olives, the black olives, and the chiles, ending with a generous topping of cheese. Sprinkle the remaining scallions and the cilantro over the cheese.

2. Cover and refrigerate several hours.

3. Serve with baskets of corn chips, pita triangles, sturdy vegetables, and crackers.

SERVES 30

18

DEVILED EGGS

Deviled eggs make great accompaniments to salads or as part of breakfast, lunch, or dinner potlucks. This recipe is undoubtedly the simplest and most popular of all egg interpretations.

12 eggs
1/3 cup whole egg mayonnaise or salad dressing, divided
3/4 teaspoon ground dry mustard
1 teaspoon minced fresh parsley leaves
pinch salt
1/4 teaspoon white pepper

1. Place the eggs in a saucepan and cover with water at least 1 inch above the eggs. Bring to a boil over moderately high heat, reduce the heat to a simmer, and cook for 2 minutes. Cover, remove the pan from the heat, and let sit for 15 minutes.

2. Place a colander in a bowl filled with ice water. Pour the eggs into the colander, deliberately banging them together to crack the shells. Change the water to keep it cool and to lower the temperature of the eggs. Leave the unpeeled eggs in the colander.

3. Begin removing the shells by cracking the pointed end, then the flat end, then rolling the eggs on the counter. Carefully peel off the shells and discard. For stubborn shells that seem glued to the egg, gently nudge the tip of a teaspoon with the spoon turned down under the shell to lift it off. Place the peeled eggs on a flat plate.

4. Slice the peeled eggs in half lengthwise. Transfer the yolks to a bowl.

5. Add most of the mayonnaise, mustard, parsley, salt, and pepper to the yolks and mash with a fork until well combined and almost smooth. Add mayonnaise by 1/2 teaspoonfuls to arrive at the right consistency.

6. Mound the filling into the egg whites. Make wavy lines with a fork in an upward direction. Sprinkle lightly with paprika or place a small parsley leaf or a sliced olive on each deviled egg. Alternatively, place the filling in a pastry bag fitted with a large star tip and pipe the filling into the egg whites.

MAKES 24

SPINACH-STUFFED MUSHROOM CASSEROLE

A combination of mushrooms and seasoned creamy spinach is made all the easier with a frozen spinach soufflé. Prepare these ahead of time, cover, and refrigerate until you're ready for them.

    1 package (12 ounces) frozen spinach soufflé
    1/4 teaspoon garlic salt, or more if desired
    dash or two hot pepper sauce
    1/3 cup shredded mozzarella cheese
    1 pound fresh large button (or white) mushrooms
    unsalted butter, melted
    1/3 cup grated Parmesan cheese

1. Partially defrost the soufflé and transfer it to a medium bowl. Mix with the garlic salt, hot pepper sauce, and mozzarella cheese; set aside.

2. Preheat the oven to 400°F. Lightly butter a shallow 2 1/2-quart casserole and set aside.

3. Remove the stems from the mushrooms and set aside for another use. Clean the mushrooms with a soft vegetable brush and damp paper towels; pat dry. Slice off a thin strip of mushroom (an o-ring) from the cap to create a larger opening for the filling. If a mushroom is uneven and tips or wobbles, remove a sliver from the bottom to keep it upright. Brush the mushrooms with the butter.

4. Fill each mushroom cap with the soufflé filling. Place the mushrooms in the prepared casserole and sprinkle with the Parmesan cheese.

5. Bake 15 minutes or until the filling is bubbly.

MAKES 20

KATHERINE'S CHILI NON-CARNE CASSEROLE DIP

Colleague and diet guru to the famous and powerful in Washington, DC, Katherine Tallmadge is the author of the best-selling *Diet Simple: 192 Mental Tricks, Substitutions, Habits and Inspirations*. Katherine serves her meatless chili dip accompanied by fresh tomato salsa, light sour cream, and guacamole.

    1/2 cup cracked wheat or bulgur
    1/2 cup boiling water or bouillon
    1 large onion, chopped
    3 large cloves garlic, minced
    1 tablespoon vegetable or olive oil
    3 tablespoons hot chile powder
    1 large green bell pepper, chopped
    1 28-ounce can whole plum tomatoes, chopped
    1 16-ounce can kidney beans
    2 jalapeño peppers, seeded and chopped (optional)
    salt and black pepper, to taste

1. Soak the cracked wheat in the water 15 minutes.

2. Sauté the onion and garlic in the oil in a large pot over moderately low heat about 15 minutes or until soft. Stir in the chile powder and simmer a few minutes. Add the green pepper and cook a few seconds. Stir in the tomatoes, kidney beans, and jalapeños, if using. Add the cracked wheat.

3. Simmer over moderately low heat until the flavors are blended and the vegetables are tender. Add additional water or bouillon to keep the ingredients moist. Season with salt and pepper.

4. Serve hot with pita triangles, flat bread, fresh vegetables, and chips.

SERVES AT LEAST 6

TAMMY AND THERESA'S SLOW COOKER ROASTED RED PEPPER AND GARLIC TOSTINIS

Tammy Biber and Theresa Howell shared this recipe from their new book, *Southwest Slow Cooking*. I met them when they were guests on my radio program. Tostinis means "little toasts" in Spanish.

2 tablespoons olive oil, divided
1 head garlic
2 red bell peppers, seeded and quartered
1 French baguette, cut into 1/4-inch slices
salt and black pepper, to taste
1/2 cup crumbled feta or Mexican cheese

1. Lightly coat the bottom of a slow cooker with 1 teaspoon of oil. Cut the top off the head of garlic; discard the top. Place the entire head in the center of the cooker.

2. Stack the bell peppers along the edges of the bottom of the cooker. Drizzle the remaining olive oil over the garlic and peppers. Cover and cook on low 5 hours.

3. Preheat the oven to 350°F. Place the slices of bread on an ungreased cookie sheet. Squeeze 1 clove of the roasted garlic on each slice of bread, spreading it across the surface.

4. Slice the red peppers and distribute them equally over each slice of bread. Season each piece with salt and pepper and top with cheese.

5. Bake the tostinis 10 minutes or until the cheese begins to melt. Serve immediately.

SERVES 16

ITALIAN MEATBALL SOUP

A hearty soup, featuring smaller -than-usual meatballs braised in a tomato-based broth, makes a satisfying, warming dish at soup potlucks.

5 cloves garlic, divided

1 1/2 to 2 pounds lean ground beef

3 large eggs, beaten

1/3 cup grated Parmesan cheese

2 tablespoons water

3/4 cup unseasoned dried bread crumbs

1/2 teaspoon salt

1 tablespoon plus 1/2 cup chopped parsley, divided

2 beef bouillon cubes

2 cups boiling water

3 carrots, pared and cut into thin rounds

3 ribs celery with leaves, thinly sliced

1 28-ounce can whole tomatoes, undrained and crushed

1 14.5-ounce can stewed tomatoes, crushed

1 envelope dry onion soup mix

1/4 teaspoon black pepper

2 teaspoons Italian seasoning

3 to 4 tablespoons olive oil

1 head escarole or curly endive, cleaned and
   cut into small pieces

1/4 cup small pasta such as elbow, shell,
   or ditalini, cooked and drained

1. Finely mince 2 cloves garlic. Combine with the beef, eggs, cheese, water, bread crumbs, salt, and 1 tablespoon parsley in a large bowl. Mix lightly but thoroughly to combine. Roll by rounded tablespoons into 30 to 35 meatballs. Refrigerate 30 minutes.

2. Dissolve the bouillon cubes in the water and set aside. Place the carrots and celery in the bottom of a slow cooker. Cover with the tomatoes, bouillon, onion soup mix, pepper, and Italian seasoning. Cover and set at high.

3. Slice the remaining 3 cloves of garlic and place in a large skillet with the oil over moderately high heat. Cook the garlic until it turns light golden; remove and discard. Lightly brown the meatballs in the oil on all sides. Remove the meatballs using a slotted spoon and place in the cooker. Continue until all the meatballs are browned and in the cooker. Cover and cook on high 5 to 6 hours.

4. Stir in the escarole 1 hour before serving. Add the pasta and remaining parsley 10 minutes before serving.

SERVES 8 TO 10

TIP: All slow cookers have individual quirks, even those of the same brand and style. My Rival 6-quart slow cooker heats up very slowly; my same-size West Bend is the fastest-heating slow cooker in the West. The moral of the story: know your slow cooker.

SLOW COOKER MINESTRONE SOUP

Minestrone means "a big, thick vegetable soup." Add whatever vegetables you have on hand to make it your own; that's the Italian way.

5 chicken or vegetable bouillon cubes

3 cups boiling water

3 tablespoons olive oil

1 cup thinly sliced onion

2 ribs celery, sliced

2 cloves garlic, minced

1 cup frozen or fresh-cut green beans

5 carrots, pared and sliced

1 small head (2 cups) cabbage, quartered,
    cored, and thinly sliced

2 14.5-ounce cans stewed tomatoes, undrained
    and crushed

2 large tomatoes, chopped

2 medium red potatoes, scrubbed and cut into eighths

1 1-pound can cannellini or navy beans

1 bay leaf

1 teaspoon salt

1/4 cup elbow macaroni, cooked al dente (optional)

freshly grated Parmesan cheese, for garnish

1. Dissolve bouillon cubes in water and set aside.

2. Warm the olive oil in a large skillet. Add the onions, celery, garlic, green beans, and carrots. Cook, stirring often, until the onions soften.

3. Layer the cabbage, stewed tomatoes, tomatoes, potatoes, cannellini beans, bay leaf, and salt in a slow cooker. Add the skillet contents and enough bouillon to come 1 inch above the vegetables. Cover and cook on high 2 hours. Lower the temperature and cook on low 3 hours.

4. Add macaroni, if using, and cook 20 to 30 minutes.

5. Pass a bowl of Parmesan cheese with the soup.

SERVES AT LEAST 8

SLOW COOKER CAULIFLOWER VEGETABLE SOUP

Filled with nutrition from cruciferous cauliflower, beta carotene-rich carrots, and potassium-dense celery and beans, this low-calorie soup warms from the inside out and is ready at just the right temperature when you want it. Now that's convenient.

4 vegetable or chicken bouillon cubes

6 cups boiling water

3 tablespoons vegetable oil

1 large onion, chopped

2 cloves garlic, minced

3 plump carrots, trimmed, pared, and sliced into rounds

3 ribs celery, trimmed and thinly sliced

1 head cauliflower, trimmed and cut into 3 to 4 cups florets

1 10-ounce package frozen butter beans or lima beans, partially defrosted

1/3 cup chopped parsley leaves and stems

salt and black pepper, to taste

dash hot sauce (optional)

2 cups hot cooked rice

1. Dissolve bouillon cubes in water and set aside.

2. Warm the oil in a large deep skillet over moderate heat. Sauté the onion and garlic until soft. Add the carrots and celery; cook 5 minutes. Add the cauliflower and toss with the vegetables until combined and coated with oil. Transfer the mixture to a slow cooker turned to high. Stir in the bouillon. Cover and cook at high 2 hours.

3. Reduce the heat to low and cook 5 to 6 hours.

4. Uncover the cooker and stir in the butter beans, salt, and pepper. Turn the heat to high and cook 45 minutes or until all the vegetables are tender.

5. Just before serving, stir in the parsley and a dash of hot sauce, if using. Serve piping hot with rice on the side.

SERVES 6 TO 8

TIP: I prefer serving the rice on the side because its thickening potential is unpredictable and leftovers may sour more quickly with it as a component.

SLOW COOKER FISH STEW

A delightful combination makes this stew marvelous dining. Enjoy toasted baguette slices with it and all's well with your world.

3 tablespoons vegetable oil

1 medium onion, chopped

2 medium carrots, pared and sliced

2 ribs celery, sliced

1 clove garlic, minced

2 medium potatoes, peeled, quartered, and sliced

2 14.5-ounce cans stewed tomatoes, cut up

1 8-ounce bottle clam juice

2 6 1/2-ounce cans chopped or minced clams, drained and
   liquid reserved

1/2 cup water

1 bay leaf

2 teaspoons salt

1/2 teaspoon black pepper

1 1/4 pounds cod fillets, cut into 1-inch pieces

1 pound large shrimp, uncooked and shelled

1/4 cup chopped parsley leaves

1. Warm the oil in a large skillet over moderate heat. Sauté the onion, carrots, celery, garlic, and potatoes until soft. Stir in the tomatoes, the bottled and reserved clam juice, water, bay leaf, salt, and pepper.

2. Transfer mixture to a slow cooker with the heat turned to high. Cover and cook 30 minutes on high.

3. Stir the ingredients, cover, and cook on low 6 to 7 hours or until the potatoes are fork-tender.

4. Stir in the clams, fish, shrimp, and parsley. Cover and cook 20 to 30 minutes or until the fish and shrimp are cooked. Serve piping hot.

SERVES AT LEAST 6

TIPS: If you're hesitant about cooking fish and seafood, trust the slow cooker to do it perfectly. This recipe calls for cod, but use any available firm chunky whitefish such as haddock or monkfish.

SLOW COOKER MEATBALLS AND LIL' DOGGIES IN A TANGY SAUCE

A combination of unlikely ingredients produces a great-tasting appetizer.

   1 10-ounce jar grape jelly
   1 12-ounce bottle cocktail sauce
   1 pound lean ground beef or round
   1 small onion, grated
   1 large egg, beaten
   1/3 to 1/2 cup unseasoned dried bread crumbs
   pinch salt
   1 1-pound package cocktail hot dogs or 1/2 pound
      regular hot dogs, cut into bite-size pieces
   2 tablespoons instant minced onion

1. Position a rack in the upper third of the oven. Preheat the oven to 450°F. Lightly oil a 9 x 13-inch baking pan and set aside.

2. Oil the slow cooker pot. Combine the jelly and sauce in the slow cooker on low heat. Cover and warm through while preparing the meatballs.

3. Combine the meat, onion, egg, bread crumbs, and salt. Mix lightly using two forks. Shape into at least 24 1/2- to 1-inch meatballs and place in the prepared baking pan. Bake 10 to 15 minutes until cooked through and lightly brown all over, shaking the pan once before turning them over.

4. Transfer the meatballs and hot dogs to the sauce. Stir in the instant minced onion. Cover and cook 3 to 4 hours. Serve hot from the pot with toothpicks.

MAKES AT LEAST 24

TIPS: Dampen your fingers before rolling the meatballs to minimize the meat's stickiness. You can use just meatballs or only doggies. If time is short, use 1 bag of frozen meatballs instead of making your own. These are already cooked, so allow them to defrost 30 minutes at room temperature before adding them to the sauce, or follow package directions.

CRABMEAT CASSEROLE

These ingredients transform into one of the best hot appetizer dips ever devised.

   8-ounces cream cheese, softened
   1 tablespoon milk
   2 teaspoons Worcestershire sauce
   1/4 cup mayonnaise
   6 to 8-ounces crabmeat, drained, juice reserved, and picked over for cartilage
   1 scallion, trimmed and finely chopped
   1/2 teaspoon creamy horseradish, or to taste
   1/4 teaspoon salt
   pinch black pepper
   2 tablespoons finely minced parsley
   1/4 cup unseasoned dried bread crumbs
   1 tablespoon unsalted butter, melted

1. Preheat the oven to 350°F. Butter a 1 1/2-quart chafing dish, soufflé dish, or 9-inch pie dish and set aside.

2. Combine the cream cheese, milk, Worcestershire sauce, mayonnaise, and crabmeat juice in a medium bowl. Gently fold in the crabmeat, scallion, horseradish, salt, pepper, and parsley. Transfer to the prepared baking dish.

3. Combine the bread crumbs with the butter and sprinkle over the crab mixture. Bake 20 minutes or until the ingredients are bubbly and the crumbs are golden brown. Serve with assorted crackers.

SERVES 8

TIPS: For convenience and flavor, I use vacuum-packed crabmeat from the fresh seafood section of my supermarket. Handle crabmeat gently when combining with the cream cheese mixture so it does not break into tiny pieces. A few tablespoons of toasted slivered almonds make a nice crunchy topping.

CLAM DIP IN A BREAD CASSEROLE

This excellent dip comes in its own edible casserole. After your guests have finished the dip, cut the clam dip-seasoned bread into slices and enjoy it with a bowl of hearty vegetable soup. Dry the hollowed loaf overnight uncovered at room temperature before filling with the dip.

1 loaf unsliced round rye bread or other unsliced round loaf

3 6 1/2-ounce cans minced clams, well drained with juice reserved and divided

2 8-ounce packages cream cheese, softened

2 tablespoons snipped fresh chives

1 clove garlic, minced

2 tablespoons fresh lemon juice

1 tablespoon Worcestershire sauce

dash hot pepper sauce (optional)

1/4 teaspoon salt

1/3 cup chopped fresh parsley

1. Hollow out the bread using a sharp, long-bladed knife, leaving a 1 1/2- to 2-inch rim around the edges. Cube the bread taken from the center and transfer to a plastic bag. Dry the hollowed loaf overnight at room temperature.

2. Preheat the oven to 275°F.

3. Mix the clams with half the reserved juice, cream cheese, chives, garlic, lemon juice, Worcestershire sauce, hot pepper sauce, if using, salt, and parsley. If the mixture is too thick, add droplets of hot water. Transfer the mixture to the hollowed loaf.

4. Wrap loaf loosely in foil and place on a baking sheet. Bake 2 1/2 hours. Transfer to a serving tray by sliding two large spatulas underneath the loaf at opposite sides. Unwrap loaf and surround with reserved bread chunks, crackers, and cucumber rounds.

SERVES AT LEAST 12

EGG SALAD SPREAD

This is a building-block recipe for egg salad; add chopped olives, chopped bell peppers, or sweet relish. Deviled ham or a small can of drained tuna makes a tasty enhancement.

> 3/4 to 1 cup (about 2 ribs) chopped celery
>
> 2 scallions, trimmed and chopped
>
> 12 hard-cooked eggs
>
> 1 cup whole egg mayonnaise
>
> 1/2 teaspoon ground dry mustard
>
> 1/4 teaspoon salt
>
> 1/4 teaspoon black pepper

1. Pulse the celery and scallions in the workbowl of a food processor. Add the eggs and pulse three times. Add the mayonnaise, mustard, salt, and pepper. Combine and pulse again to coarsely chop the eggs.

2. Transfer the mixture to a bowl, cover, and refrigerate until needed.

SERVES 12 TO 15

TIP: Ground dry mustard is a potent seasoning; a little goes a long way.

hether it's a potluck party after a concert or friends getting together to start the day, with these casserole recipes you'll be prepared for every occasion. They adjust to your schedule because they do superbly well made ahead of time, leaving you relaxed and ready to enjoy the event. Select from these outstanding preparations – winners at any time – as main courses, complements, or sweet finales, and accompany them with champagne, orange juice, or coffee.

DALIA'S OVERNIGHT ORANGE PULL-APART SWEET ROLLS

My cousin Dalia knows exactly what to serve at all times, and folks rave about everything she makes. Refrigerate the rolls 18 to 24 hours before baking.

> 1/2 cup unsalted butter
> 1 cup commercially prepared cream cheese frosting
> 1 3.4-ounce box instant vanilla pudding mix
> 24 frozen dinner rolls, defrosted
> 1/4 cup golden raisins
> zest from 1 large navel orange

1. Lightly butter and flour a 9- or 10-inch fluted tube pan and set aside.

2. Melt the butter with the cream cheese frosting and set aside.

3. Place the pudding mix on a sheet of wax paper. Cut the rolls in half. Coat each half in the pudding mix and place in the bottom of the prepared pan. Sprinkle with a few raisins and the orange zest. Continue until all rolls are used. Sprinkle the remaining pudding mix and zest on the rolls.

4. Slowly pour the butter and frosting combination over the rolls. Cover tightly with plastic wrap and refrigerate 18 to 24 hours.

5. Preheat the oven to 350°F. Uncover the rolls. Bake 30 to 35 minutes or until the rolls are golden and a tester inserted in several places comes out clean.

SERVES 18 TO 24

TIP: Removing only the rind or zest from citrus is a cinch when you have the proper tools. Two devices, the microplane and the French zester, are inexpensive and available in kitchen shops. The microplane grates tiny dots of zest and almost guarantees leaving the bitter white pith on the orange; the French zester removes wispy threads of rind. You can always use a handheld box grater or a vegetable peeler.

PUFFY CHEESE STRATA WITH VARIATIONS

Strata originated with the Latin word *sternere*, which means "to layer one material on another." Cheese strata originated in the throes of the food rationing days during World War II. Devised by home economists, it provided families with high-quality nourishment using ordinary, available ingredients. Even today it's still popular. Note that it must be refrigerated overnight before baking.

15 slices fresh bread, crusts trimmed

unsalted butter, softened

3 cups shredded swiss or cheddar cheese

8 large eggs

4 cups whole milk

2 teaspoons grated onion or shallot

2 teaspoons Dijon mustard

1 2-ounce jar pimentos, drained

3 tablespoons grated Parmesan cheese

1. Butter a 9 x 13-inch baking dish and set aside. Butter the bread, cut each slice into 12 cubes, and pack the cubes into the bottom of the prepared dish. Distribute the shredded cheese over the bread.

2. Whisk the eggs with the milk, onion, and mustard; stir in the pimentos. Pour the liquid mixture over the bread. Cover and refrigerate overnight.

3. Preheat the oven to 350°F.

4. Sprinkle the strata with the Parmesan cheese. Bake 50 to 60 minutes or until golden brown and puffy and a knife inserted in the center comes out clean. If the top becomes brown too soon, loosely tent with foil until done.

SERVES 8 TO 10

TIP: Create different strata by using other ingredients such as cooked, drained, and crumbled sausage; ham slivers; or cooked vegetables. Add crabmeat combined with cooked asparagus, or chopped spinach with cooked fresh mushrooms and swiss cheese.

SALLY'S CORNED BEEF HASH CASSEROLE

My friend Sally serves this for breakfast, lunch, and dinner — actually, whenever the spirit moves her — and she accompanies it with dishes suitable for the time of day. I have found similar recipes in numerous regional fund-raising cookbooks; it's a perennial favorite.

8 ounces noodles

1 tablespoon unsalted butter

2 medium onions, chopped

1/2 cup chopped green bell pepper

1 10 3/4-ounce can cream of mushroom soup, undiluted

1 cup whole milk

3/4 cup grated or shredded cheddar cheese

1 15-ounce can corned beef hash

3/4 cup bread crumbs

3 tablespoons unsalted butter, melted

1. Preheat the oven to 350°F. Butter a 2 1/2-quart casserole and set aside.

2. Cook the noodles 5 minutes in boiling salted water. Place the noodles in a colander and drain well by shaking it. Place the noodles in the prepared casserole.

3. Melt the butter in a large skillet over moderate heat. Sauté the onions and green pepper until softened. Stir in the soup, milk, and cheese and cook over moderately low heat until the cheese melts. Remove the pan from the heat and mix in the corned beef hash. Pour the mixture into the casserole and combine with the noodles.

4. Combine the bread crumbs and melted butter in a small bowl and sprinkle over the top of the casserole.

5. Bake 30 to 35 minutes or until the ingredients are bubbly and the crumbs are golden brown.

SERVES 6 TO 8

TIP: Try the different brands of corned beef hash available in supermarkets to see which you prefer. The meat-to-potato ratio is different for each. For a favorite side dish, try fresh pineapple cubes mixed with sliced strawberries.

EGG-IN-A-HOLE

My kids were crazy about eggs prepared this way, and they've continued the tradition with their children, who, in turn, are crazy about them, too. A team effort always pays off: Enlist a helper, especially when it comes to breaking the eggs and cooking them. These are so good that you'll be surprised how many little kids pack away. These are great for a church breakfast.

unsalted butter, softened and divided

2 slices bread per person

2 large eggs per person

CONTINUED >

1. Preheat the oven to 300°F. Spread butter generously on one side of each slice of bread. Cut a hole from the center of each slice with a 1 1/2-inch biscuit cutter and set aside.

2. Melt 1 tablespoon of butter in a skillet or on a griddle over moderate heat until it bubbles. Toast the bread circles on both sides in the skillet and set aside on a baking sheet in the oven with the door slightly ajar. Melt more butter in the skillet until it bubbles.

3. Place the unbuttered side of the bread in the hot butter and cook 1 to 2 minutes or until lightly toasted. While the bread is toasting, break an egg into a custard cup for each slice of bread in the skillet. Turn the bread over using a spatula. Carefully slip the egg from the cup into the hole, keeping the yolk intact. Cook until the egg is set, 2 or more minutes.

4. Carefully turn the egg over using a spatula, and cook about 1 minute so it is cooked over easy. Cook longer if you prefer egg yolks more set. Repeat with the remaining toast and eggs, adding more butter as needed. Remove the fried bread rounds from the oven.

5. Alternatively, place each toasted bread and egg on a buttered baking sheet and place in the warm oven with the door closed to complete cooking. This eliminates turning the egg over and is especially handy when you have many to cook.

6. Serve hot or warm with fried bread rounds.

Serves 2 per person

FRUIT-FILLED BREAD PUDDING

One of the best dishes in the world is bread pudding. Its origins may be humble, but the combined textures and flavors make it divine. When I have pannetone or Columba de Pasqua left from the holidays, I usually reduce it to crumbs and make a memorable pudding.

> 10 cups raisin bread crumbs
> 1 tablespoon ground cinnamon
> 1 to 2 cups assorted dried fruits, chopped or snipped
> 1 1/2 cups heavy cream
> 1 1/2 cups evaporated milk
> 1 cup sugar
> 3 large eggs
> 4 tablespoons unsalted butter, melted

1. Preheat the oven to 350°F. Butter the bottom and sides of a 9 x 13-inch casserole and set aside.

2. Combine the bread crumbs with the cinnamon and dried fruits in a large bowl.

3. Beat the cream, milk, sugar, and eggs together until well combined. Pour over the dry ingredients and lightly mix until everything is wet.

4. Transfer the mixture to the prepared casserole. Bake 1 hour or until a knife inserted in several places comes out clean.

5. Remove pudding from oven. Increase temperature to 375°F. Drizzle the butter over the pudding. Return the pudding to the oven and bake 15 to 20 minutes or until the top is golden brown. Serve warm or hot with whipped cream or soft vanilla ice cream.

SERVES 12

TIPS: This pudding is delicious baked immediately after mixing it. You can also put it in the refrigerator overnight and bake it the next morning.

JUDITH FERTIG'S CORNHUSKER'S CASSEROLE

A few years ago at an Association of Food Journalists (AFJ) conference in Kansas City, I met Judith Fertig. Since then, she's been a guest on my radio show several times. When I asked her for a potluck-type recipe, she quickly responded with this one. This brunch dish features both corn and hominy, and comes from her book, *Prairie Home Cooking*. It was served to the AFJ attendees for a Thanksgiving lunch at The American Restaurant.

2 cups yellow and or white hominy, drained and patted dry
2 cups fresh or frozen (and thawed) sweet corn
1 clove garlic, cut into small pieces
8 ounces sharp Wisconsin cheddar cheese, shredded
2 cups whole milk
4 large eggs, beaten
1 teaspoon salt
1/4 teaspoon ground red pepper

1. Preheat the oven to 350°F. Butter a 9 x 13-inch baking dish.

2. Mix the hominy and corn together in the baking dish. Combine the garlic and cheddar cheese and sprinkle over the top.

3. Whisk together the milk, eggs, salt, and pepper together in a large measuring cup or bowl. Pour the mixture over the corn.

4. Bake 50 to 60 minutes or until bubbling and set. Allow casserole to settle 10 minutes before serving.

SERVES 8 TO 10

SAUSAGE-FILLED CORNBREAD WITH A SIDE OF SAUTEED APPLES

The combination of sausage and cornbread with a side of sautéed apples is the classic trinity of a Southern breakfast. This rendition is a little unusual and great for potlucks.

2 pounds bulk pork sausage

3 large eggs

4 tablespoons unsalted butter, melted and cooled

1 1/4 cups half-and-half or regular evaporated milk

1 cup yellow cornmeal

1 cup all-purpose flour

1 tablespoon sugar

2 1/4 teaspoons baking powder

1 teaspoon salt

Sautéed Apples (see recipe right)

1. Preheat the oven to 375°F. Lightly butter a shallow 9 x 13-inch baking dish and set aside.

2. Cook the sausage in a skillet over moderate heat until thoroughly cooked, breaking up the large pieces. Drain and pat dry.

3. Whisk together the eggs, butter, and half-and-half or evaporated milk in a large bowl. Combine the cornmeal, flour, sugar, baking powder, and salt in another bowl. Whisk the dry ingredients into the wet ingredients until well combined and the batter is smooth. Fold the sausage into the batter. Transfer the batter into the prepared baking dish.

4. Bake 25 to 30 minutes or until a tester inserted in the center comes out clean. Allow the ingredients to settle about 10 minutes before cutting into squares.

SERVES 10 TO 12

TIP: This cornbread makes a fine accompaniment to soups, salads, and omelets.

SAUTÉED APPLES

4 tablespoons unsalted butter

1/2 to 3/4 cup pure maple syrup

1 to 2 teaspoons ground cinnamon (optional)

5 cups peeled, cored, thinly sliced apples

1. Melt the butter in a large skillet and add the maple syrup, blending the two ingredients. Stir in the cinnamon, if using.

2. Add the apples and cook, tossing them about, over moderately high heat until seasoned and soft, about 15 minutes. Serve hot with the casserole.

MAKES ABOUT 4 CUPS

CINNAMON RAISIN HONEY BUNS

These buns are as easy to prepare as they are scrumptious to eat.

Rolls:
3/4 cup hot water
1/4 cup honey
1 16-ounce box hot roll mix
1 large egg, blended
2 tablespoons unsalted butter, softened

Filling:
2 tablespoons unsalted butter, melted
2 tablespoons honey
1/2 cup firmly packed light brown sugar
1 1/2 to 2 teaspoons ground cinnamon
1/3 cup raisins, softened

Icing:
1 1/4 cups confectioners' sugar
3 to 4 tablespoons milk or cream

1. Spread vegetable shortening over a 9 x 13-inch baking pan and set aside.

2. To make the rolls, combine hot water with honey. Prepare the hot roll mix, adding the water and honey mixture instead of plain water and incorporating the egg and butter according to the box instructions. Cover the dough and allow to rise 45 minutes.

3. To make the filling, combine the butter and honey in a cup. Combine the sugar, cinnamon, and raisins in a small bowl.

4. Roll the dough into a 20 x 12-inch rectangle on a lightly floured work surface. Brush the butter-honey mixture over all the dough. Sprinkle the sugar-raisin mixture over it, patting down gently.

5. Roll the dough tightly from a long side, making certain there are no air pockets. Pinch the seams closed. Cut the roll into 14 to 16 slices. Place the rolls cut side down in the prepared pan, shaping them, if necessary, into a round shape. Preheat the oven to 350°F.

6. Lay plastic wrap and a tea towel over the rolls. Allow them to rise in a warm spot for 30 to 45 minutes or until risen and puffy. (I usually fill a pan or bowl with very hot water and put the baking pan on top of it.)

7. Bake 30 minutes or until the rolls are a light golden brown and a tester inserted in the center comes out clean. Cool in the pan on a wire rack for 10 minutes.

8. To make the icing, mix the ingredients until thick and smooth. Drizzle or brush over the warm rolls.

SERVES 14 TO 16

OMELETS FOR A CROWD

Making a huge omelet uses many of the same methods called for when making smaller ones. This omelet is easier because after the bottom is set, the pan goes into the oven to finish cooking. Cut this omelet like a pizza, which is the name two of my grandchildren, James and Thomas, have given to giant omelets.

12 large eggs, beaten
2 tablespoons unsalted butter
2 tablespoons salad oil
1/3 cup minced fresh parsley
12 slices fresh tomato
2 cups shredded cheese of choice
1/4 cup grated Parmesan cheese (optional)

1. Preheat the oven to 350°F. Cover the skillet handle with a double wrapping of aluminum foil if it is not ovenproof.

2. Beat the eggs in a blender.

3. Warm the butter and oil in a 12-inch skillet, even if the skillet is nonstick, over moderately high heat. When the butter starts to bubble and sizzle but not brown or burn, distribute it evenly over the bottom and up the sides of the pan. When the sizzling subsides, pour the eggs into the center of the butter. Sprinkle the parsley over the eggs.

4. Use a spatula to pull the eggs from the edges toward the center, allowing the uncooked portion to flow to the edges. Continue pulling the eggs at least twice more.

5. Remove the pan from the heat. Arrange tomato slices around the edges of the omelet and distribute the shredded cheese all over the top. Sprinkle with Parmesan cheese, if using.

6. Bake 15 to 20 minutes or until the cheese is bubbly and golden brown and the omelet is fully cooked. Remove the skillet from the oven and place it on the stove or on a heat proof trivet. Allow the omelet to settle a few minutes. Cut into wedges and serve hot.

SERVES 10

TIPS: This partners with fresh fruit, lettuce salad, and plenty of soft warm rolls with butter. If using cheese, any cheese or combination of cheeses can be used, although I much prefer the kinds that melt. Omelets adapt to many ingredients, such as sausage, vegetables, and ham, as long as the ingredients are cooked or sautéed before they're added to the eggs. To make a potato omelet: Cook the sliced potatoes with onions and remove from the skillet when brown around the edges. Make the omelet, distributing the potatoes evenly over the eggs just before placing the omelet in the oven. It's not necessary, but a little shredded cheese over the potatoes adds enrichment.

DUKE'S FAVORITE CHEESE AND GREEN CHILE CASSEROLE

John Wayne liked his friends to call him "Duke," the name he adopted from his favorite Airedale terrier. The legend, as reported by one of Duke's cooks, is that this was Duke's favorite casserole and he sometimes prepared it for his guests. It makes a fine brunch dish served with a glass of champagne.

2 4-ounce cans diced green chiles, drained
2 scallions, trimmed and thinly sliced
3 cups shredded cheddar cheese
3 cups shredded Monterey Jack cheese
2 tablespoons all-purpose flour
4 large eggs, separated
2/3 cup half-and-half, cream, or evaporated milk
1/4 cup plus 2 tablespoons mayonnaise, divided
1 tablespoon yellow mustard
1/2 teaspoon sweet paprika
1/4 teaspoon salt
pinch black pepper
2 teaspoons Worcestershire sauce
3 tablespoons cornflake crumbs
1 tablespoon unsalted butter, melted
2 medium tomatoes, cut into half-moon slices

1. Preheat the oven to 325°F. Butter a 2 1/2-quart casserole and set aside.

2. Combine the chiles and scallions with both cheeses and flour in the prepared casserole.

3. Beat the egg whites in a large bowl until stiff peaks form. Set aside.

4. Using the same beaters, beat egg yolks, half-and-half, 1/4 cup mayonnaise, mustard, paprika, salt, pepper, and Worcestershire in another large bowl.

5. Fold the egg whites into the egg yolk mixture. Pour slowly into the cheese mixture and combine, using a fork and shaking the dish occasionally to allow the liquids to trickle into the cheese.

6. Combine the cornflake crumbs with the butter and sprinkle over the top. Bake 30 minutes.

7. Remove the casserole and smear the remaining 2 tablespoons mayonnaise on the top. Arrange the tomatoes, slightly overlapping, around the edges of the casserole. Bake 30 minutes or until a knife inserted in the center comes out clean. Allow the casserole to settle 10 minutes before cutting.

SERVES AT LEAST 10

TIP: Large tomato slices cut into half moons look attractive around the edges of the casserole. If you are using smaller Roma tomatoes, however, leave the slices whole.

BEEF, PORK, AND LAMB ENTRÉES

Presenting delicious dishes from around the world make potlucks more interesting. This chapter includes a wealth of dishes, including typical all-American preparations such as the classic California Casserole; Sloppy Joes (aka Virginia Spoon Burgers), the youngsters' favorite dish; Beef and Macaroni Casserole in two variations; Maria's Moussaka with its Greek and Middle Eastern origins; Lion's Head, an unusual Chinese meatball dish; and the St. Patty's Day favorite, Slow Cooker Corned Beef and Cabbage. These recipes take everyday ingredients and turn them into beautiful, tasty dishes.

LION'S HEAD

I first had this meatball dish at a Chinese restaurant my mother took me to in Paterson, New Jersey. This dish often has many more seasonings than I have listed.

4 chicken bouillon cubes

1 1/2 cups boiling water

1 1/2 pounds ground pork

3 cloves garlic, finely minced

3 scallions, trimmed and finely sliced

1 1-inch piece gingerroot, peeled and grated

1 large egg, beaten

5 to 6 tablespoons soy sauce, divided

5 tablespoons cornstarch, more as necessary

4 tablespoons peanut or corn oil, divided

1 pound cabbage (Chinese or napa) washed, drained, and shredded

2 tablespoons dry sherry

2 tablespoons sesame oil

1 bunch fresh spinach, cleaned, stemmed, and shredded

4 cups cooked white rice

1. Dissolve bouillon cubes in water and set aside.

2. Mix the pork, garlic, scallions, gingerroot, egg, and 3 tablespoons soy sauce in a large bowl until thoroughly combined. Shape 3 tablespoons of the mixture into a meatball. Make all meatballs the same size. (They can be smaller, but they are typically large.) Place them on wax paper and roll them in the cornstarch. Set aside.

3. Preheat the oven to 325°F. Lightly oil a deep 4-quart casserole with a lid or a 9 x 13-inch baking dish that will be covered with aluminum foil.

4. Place the peanut oil in a wok or large skillet over moderately high heat and tilt to spread the oil. Heat the oil until a few drops of water dropped onto the surface dance and disappear quickly. Place a few meatballs in the wok and cook, turning them until golden brown all over. Place them on a dish. Continue until all the meatballs are brown.

5. Place the cabbage in the wok and toss it to coat with the oil. Transfer the cabbage to the prepared casserole. Place the meatballs on top of the cabbage.

6. Whisk the bouillon with the sherry in a bowl. Pour over the meatballs and cabbage. Drizzle the sesame oil and remaining 2 or 3 tablespoons soy sauce over the cabbage and meatballs.

7. Cover the casserole and bake 45 minutes. Uncover and add the spinach over the meatballs. Cover and bake 10 to 15 minutes. Serve from the casserole accompanied by white rice, with additional soy sauce on the table for seasoning.

SERVES 8 TO 10

MARIA'S MOUSSAKA

My daughter-in-law Maria entered our family bearing the delicious gifts of Greek cooking. "Moussaka is prepared different ways," she explains, "but layers of broiled or fried eggplant are constant. The classic meat — lamb — could give way to beef or veal, and the topping may be plain yogurt combined with a Greek melting cheese, or different kinds of white sauce. It depends on what the cook wants to do and what's on hand."

2 pounds eggplant, trimmed, peeled, and cut
    into 1/4-inch slices
olive oil plus 2 tablespoons, divided
1 large onion, peeled and diced
1 1/2 pounds lean ground lamb, beef, or veal
1 1/2 teaspoons ground cinnamon
1/4 to 1/2 teaspoon cayenne
1 8-ounce can tomato sauce
1/4 cup chopped parsley leaves
salt and black pepper, to taste
1/2 cup grated Parmesan cheese, divided
1/2 cup shredded white cheddar or Greek cooking
    cheese such as *kefalotiri*, divided
White Sauce (see recipe page 43)

1. Position the oven rack 4 inches below the broiler and turn the broiler to high setting.

2. Place the eggplant slices on a broiler pan. Brush each slice with the oil. Reduce the broiler temperature to low. Broil the slices until lightly brown. Turn the slices over and broil the other side. Remove from the oven and set aside.

3. Warm the remaining 2 tablespoons of oil in a large skillet and cook the onion with the meat, browning the meat until no longer pink and breaking up the large pieces. Place the meat in a strainer; drain the excess fat. Wipe out the skillet. Increase the heat to moderately high and return the meat and onions to the skillet. When the ingredients begin to sizzle, stir in the cinnamon and cayenne, add the tomato sauce, and cook 15 minutes at a high simmer. Turn off heat, stir in parsley, and season with salt and pepper.

4. Preheat the oven to 350°F. Lightly oil a 9 x 13-inch casserole. Place a slightly overlapping layer of eggplant slices in the bottom of the casserole. Sprinkle with 3 tablespoons of each cheese. Cover the cheeses with the meat mixture. Place the remaining eggplant slices over the meat. Blanket the eggplant with the white sauce. Sprinkle the remaining cheeses over the white sauce.

5. Bake 45 minutes or until the topping is golden brown. Allow the moussaka to settle 15 minutes before serving.

SERVES 12

WHITE SAUCE

3 tablespoons unsalted butter
3 tablespoons all-purpose flour
2 cups whole milk, warmed
salt and black pepper, to taste
2 egg yolks, beaten (optional)

1. Melt the butter in a medium saucepan over moderate heat and whisk in the flour until smooth. Remove from the heat and whisk in the milk. Return to the heat and cook while stirring until the sauce bubbles and thickens.

2. If using the egg yolks, place a cupful of sauce in a bowl and whisk in the egg yolk. Return to the saucepan and cook while stirring until smooth and thickened.

MAKES ABOUT 2 1/2 CUPS

TIP: Traditionally, egg yolks are a part of the white sauce. However, they sometimes curdle if the temperature isn't exactly correct when they're added. I often omit the egg yolks, and the dish remains exceptional.

EILEEN'S OLD-FASHIONED BEEF STEW WITH POTATO DUMPLINGS

When Eileen McGrory's big family gets together for potlucks, she prepares this hearty beef stew, a specialty she's been making for years. She often adds cubes of leftover roast beef to the pot, along with any extra gravy.

8 or more beef bouillon cubes

6 or more cups boiling water

3 pounds round, chuck, or stew meat, cut
    into 1 1/2-inch cubes

8 plump carrots, scraped and diagonally cut
    into 2-inch lengths

3 medium whole onions, peeled and quartered

1 teaspoon sweet paprika

1 bay leaf

2 cups frozen green beans

1 pound button mushrooms, sliced

2 cups frozen peas

salt and black pepper, to taste

3 tablespoons instant flour

1/3 cup water

Potato Dumplings (see recipe page 45)

1. Dissolve the bouillon in the water and set aside. Place the meat in a saucepan, cover with cold water, and bring to a boil. Reduce the heat and simmer for 30 minutes. Drain and rinse off the meat. Place in a 6- to 8-quart stew pot or Dutch oven.

2. Add the carrots, onions, paprika, bay leaf, and bouillon; stir to combine. Bring to a boil over moderately high heat. Reduce the heat to moderately low and simmer 2 hours. Add the beans, mushrooms, and peas; cook 30 minutes or more until all the ingredients are tender.

3. Dissolve the flour in the water and stir into the simmering stew. Cook uncovered until thickened.

4. Preheat oven to 375°F. Prepare potato dumplings.

5. Scoop 1 tablespoon of the dumpling dough and push it into the hot stew with another spoon. Continue until all the dumplings are made, leaving a little space between each one so they don't stick together.

6. Cover the Dutch oven and place it in the oven. Bake 30 to 45 minutes or until the mixture is bubbly. Insert a toothpick into a few dumplings. If it comes out clean, the dumplings are cooked. Serve the stew in wide soup bowls.

SERVES AT LEAST 8

TIP: If the extra gravy is sufficiently thick, don't add the 3 tablespoons flour and 1/3 cup water as stated in step 3. The dumplings provide thickening power, too.

POTATO DUMPLINGS

1 1/2 cups instant mashed potatoes

1 large egg, beaten

1/2 teaspoon salt

1 teaspoon instant minced onion

2 teaspoons dried chives

1/3 cup dry plain bread crumbs

1/4 cup all-purpose flour

1/4 teaspoon baking powder

1/4 teaspoon black pepper

1. Make the potatoes according to package directions. Allow the mixture to cool slightly.

2. Combine potatoes with remaining ingredients in a medium bowl and stir vigorously to mix.

MAKES 8 TO 10 DUMPLINGS

DALIA'S SAUSAGE AND VEGETABLE STEW

Sausage and vegetables come together in this robustly flavored Italian-style meal everyone enjoys.

2 pounds Italian sausage, cut into 2-inch pieces

4 cups celery, cut into 1 1/2-inch pieces

8 medium potatoes, pared and quartered

2 medium onions, halved and sliced into half moons

3 plump carrots, pared and cut into 1 1/2-inch pieces

2 tablespoons olive oil

2 teaspoons Italian seasoning

1 medium green or red bell pepper, cut into
   1 1/2-inch triangles

parsley leaves for garnish

1. Preheat the oven to 400°F. Lightly oil a 9 x 13-inch casserole and set aside.

2. Arrange the sausage, celery, potatoes, onions, and carrots in the prepared casserole. Drizzle with the oil. Sprinkle with the Italian seasoning. Mix the ingredients with your hands.

3. Cover the dish tightly with foil. Bake 45 minutes. Uncover and turn the sausage pieces over. Distribute the peppers over the ingredients. Bake 25 to 30 minutes or until the sausages are brown and the potatoes and carrots are cooked.

4. Remove ingredients with a slotted spoon, allowing the juices to drip back into the pan, and transfer to a serving platter. Garnish with the parsley.

SERVES 8

PAM'S BLACK BEAN CHILI CON CARNE

Pam Palmer, a colleague from Southern Foodways Alliance, suggests using red kidney beans if black beans are not favored, but please use dried beans — they're crucial to the preparation. Pam's credo is basic: "Cooking is an adventure; have fun." Note that beans are prepared at least 1 day in advance of serving.

4 cups dried black beans, sorted, well rinsed, and soaked

3 to 6 tablespoons vegetable or olive oil, divided

2 large onions, chopped

2 large green bell peppers, diced

2 to 4 cloves garlic, chopped

2 tablespoons sweet Hungarian paprika

2 tablespoons ground cumin

2 tablespoons ground chile powder

1 pound ground chuck or stew meat, cut into small cubes

1 35-ounce can whole tomatoes, crushed

2 cups beef broth made with bouillon cubes, divided

1 tablespoon dried oregano leaves, crushed

1/2 teaspoon unsweetened cocoa

pinch ground cinnamon

2 4-ounce cans chopped chiles

1 16-ounce jar salsa (degree of heat is your preference)

2 teaspoons salt

Toppings:
shredded cheese, sour cream, cilantro, chopped green onions

1. Soak the beans overnight. The next day, drain the beans, place in a 10-quart pot and cover with cold water reaching 3 inches above them. Bring to a boil, reduce the heat to maintain a slow boil, cover, and cook 1 1/2 to 2 hours or until the beans are tender but still firm. Check the pot frequently for the water level and add water to keep it well above the level of the beans. When the beans are cooked, strain and reserve 1 cup of the cooking liquid. Put the beans in a cooking pot suitable for a table presentation.

2. Add 3 tablespoons of oil to a large skillet. Sauté the onions, bell peppers, and garlic with the paprika, cumin, and chile powder until soft, but not brown. Transfer to the bean pot.

3. Put 1 tablespoon of oil into the same skillet and sauté the meat over moderately high heat, incorporating any bits of vegetables and spices that may have adhered to the bottom of the pan from the previous step. Add the meat to the bean pot.

4. Add tomatoes to the bean pot with 1 cup of beef broth and the reserved 1 cup of bean liquid. Stir in the oregano, cocoa, cinnamon, chiles, salsa, and salt. Cover and simmer on low heat for 1 1/2 hours. Stir occasionally so nothing sticks to the bottom of the pot. If the mixture seems to be drying, add 1 cup of beef broth.

5. Fill bowls with the toppings and set around the bean pot. Serve the chili piping hot from the pot.

SERVES 10

SLOPPY JOES [AKA VIRGINIA SPOON BURGERS]

My children introduced me to this popular chili variation in the early 1960s. It is spooned into hamburger rolls — hence the name spoon burgers.

2 tablespoons vegetable oil

1 large yellow onion, chopped

2 plump cloves garlic, finely minced

1 large green bell pepper, chopped

1 1/2 pounds coarsely ground beef

1 14.5-ounce can stewed tomatoes, chopped

1 8-ounce can tomato sauce

6 tablespoons ketchup or tomato paste

1 14-ounce can beef broth

2 to 4 tablespoons Worcestershire sauce

2 teaspoons apple cider vinegar

salt and black pepper to taste

soft or toasted hamburger rolls

1. Warm the oil with the onion and garlic over moderately low heat in a large, deep skillet suitable for table service. Cook covered about 10 minutes, stirring a couple of times until the onions soften. Add the green pepper and cook 3 minutes while stirring. Add the meat and cook until it is no longer pink, breaking up large pieces with the side of a wooden spoon. Stir in the tomatoes, tomato sauce, ketchup, and beef broth.

2. Increase the heat to medium and bring to a boil. Reduce the heat to maintain a slow boil, partially cover, and cook about 30 minutes, stirring frequently. Add the Worcestershire sauce, vinegar, salt, and pepper; stir to blend. Simmer about 15 minutes.

3. Serve hot with toasted or soft hamburger buns.

SERVES 4 TO 6

TIPS: Ketchup adds a slightly jazzed-up flavor to the ingredients; it also has thickening properties. Tomato paste provides tomato flavor and acts as a thickening agent, too.

STEAK AND MUSHROOM PIE

I returned home from London's Le Cordon Bleu Cookery School laden with notes about the traditional English foods I prepared in classes or enjoyed in restaurants. I knew Steak and Pigeon Pie, that beloved English dish, wouldn't play well with the home folks, so I prepared this instead.

4 beef bouillon cubes

2 1/2 cups boiling water

2 1/2 pounds flank or round steak, trimmed of all fat

instant flour

1/3 cup vegetable oil, divided

1 1-pound sweet onion, such as Walla Walla,
   OSO Sweet, or Vidalia, peeled, halved, and
   sliced into thin half moons

8 ounces sliced button mushrooms

8 ounces small whole button mushrooms

1/2 teaspoon black pepper

4 tablespoons unsalted butter, melted and divided

3 tablespoons all-purpose flour

2 teaspoons dried marjoram leaves

Pastry (see recipe page 49)

1. Dissolve bouillon cubes in water and set aside.

2. Cut the meat into thin strips. Dust the meat on all sides with the flour. Warm 3 tablespoons of the oil in a large skillet and brown the meat lightly on all sides without crowding the pan. (Crowding causes the meat to steam and give off juices instead of browning.) Turn the meat using tongs until all are brown, but not crusty, adding more oil as needed. Transfer the meat as it is done to a 9 x 13-inch baking dish.

3. Add 2 tablespoons of the oil to the skillet and sauté the onions until softened. Layer the onions on top of the meat but do not mix.

4. Add the remaining oil to the skillet and sauté all the mushrooms until they give up their juices. Season with pepper and cook until the mixture is dry. Layer the mushrooms on top of the onions. Shake the baking dish back and forth to distribute the layers evenly, but don't combine them.

5. Combine 3 tablespoons of butter with the flour in the skillet over moderate heat. Cook while stirring until the mixture is golden brown. Stir in the marjoram until combined. Add the bouillon and cook, while stirring, until thickened. Pour the gravy over the baking dish ingredients.

6. Position the rack in the center of the oven and

preheat the oven to 350°F.

7. On a lightly floured surface, roll the pastry into a 15 x 12-inch, 1/4-inch thick rectangle. Using a ruler as a guide, remove 1 1/4 inches of pastry from the four sides. Press the removed pastry onto the rim of the baking dish. Fold the remaining pastry in half and cut a half-dollar-size circle from the center. Place the folded pastry over half the filling; unfold the other half of the pastry to blanket the entire filling. Lightly press the pastry firmly around the edges and pinch together to crimp. Poke holes all over the pastry with the tip of a paring knife. Brush with the remaining 1 tablespoon of butter.

8. Bake 1 1/2 to 2 hours or until the juices bubble up and the pastry is golden brown. Allow to settle for 10 minutes before spooning onto dinner plates.

SERVES 8 TO 10

TIP: Formulated to dissolve instantly in hot or cold liquids and for making smooth gravies and sauces, instant flour (Gold Medal Wondra and Pillsbury Instant Blend) is in the baking sections of supermarkets. It is not a substitute for all-purpose flour. I use instant flour to dust the meat because it gives a light coating without developing lumps or goo.

PASTRY

2 1/3 cups all-purpose flour
1/4 teaspoon salt
2/3 cup solid vegetable shortening, in small chunks
5 to 6 tablespoons cold water, or more as needed

1. Combine the flour and salt in a large bowl. Add the shortening and cut in using a pastry blender or two knives until the mixture is crumbly. Sprinkle with 4 tablespoons of water, 1 tablespoon at a time. Toss lightly with a fork until the pastry begins to come together.

2. Sprinkle in the remaining water and repeat until the dough cleans the bowl and forms a ball. Cover with plastic wrap and refrigerate.

MAKES 1 CRUST

JEFF AND ANNA'S SLOW COOKER CHINESE BARBECUED PORK

My son and his wife live in an area of endless potlucks. Tables are set up in the curve of their cul de sac, and neighbors come bearing a different dish for each occasion.

3/4 cup unsweetened juice, such as apple or white grape juice
2 tablespoons sugar
2 tablespoons soy sauce
1 tablespoon distilled white vinegar
1 teaspoon grated fresh gingerroot or ground ginger
4 cloves garlic, finely minced
4 star anise (optional)
black pepper, to taste
3 pounds pork sirloin roast
2 tablespoons cornstarch
3 tablespoons cold water

1. Combine the juice, sugar, soy sauce, vinegar, gingerroot, garlic, star anise, if using, and pepper in a measuring cup. Set aside.

2. Score the fat on the pork roast in a crosshatch pattern. Place in a slow cooker. Pour the juice mixture over the meat.

3. Cover and cook on high 1 hour. Reduce heat to low and cook 7 to 8 hours or until the meat is fork-tender.

4. Place the pork on a platter. Increase the heat to high. Combine the cornstarch and water in a measuring cup and whisk until it is smooth. Stir it into the cooker, blending it with the juice mixture. Cover and cook until the mixture thickens.

5. Pull apart the meat with two forks. Return the meat to the cooker; serve directly from the pot with soft sandwich rolls and vinegar-dressed coleslaw.

SERVES AT LEAST 8

CALIFORNIA CASSEROLE

This is real 1950s meal-in-a-dish home-style cooking. My mother and most of her friends loved making it for their casual potluck suppers. Just to be different, my mother topped hers with mozzarella cheese and called it "hacienda casserole."

2 tablespoons vegetable oil
2 cloves garlic, finely minced
1 large onion, finely minced
1 large green bell pepper, cored, seeded, and chopped
1 1/2 pounds lean ground beef or round
3 teaspoons dried oregano leaves
few red pepper flakes

2 beef bouillon cubes, crumbled
salt and black pepper, to taste
2 tablespoons Worcestershire sauce
1 1-pound can plum tomatoes, crushed
1 1-pound can white or red beans, drained and rinsed
3/4 cup uncooked rice
1/3 cup sliced green salad olives with pimento strips, drained and rinsed
3/4 to 1 cup shredded cheddar cheese

1. Preheat the oven to 350°F. Lightly oil a 9 x 13-inch casserole and set aside.

2. Warm oil in a large skillet and over moderately high heat. Add garlic, onion, and bell pepper and sauté for several minutes until the vegetables soften. Mix in meat and cook until no longer pink, breaking up the large pieces. Place the mixture in a strainer to drain off excess fat. Wipe out the skillet with paper towels and return the mixture to the skillet.

3. Stir in the oregano, red pepper flakes, bouillon, salt, pepper, Worcestershire sauce, tomatoes, beans, and rice. Stir together and cook a few minutes.

4. Transfer the mixture to the prepared casserole. Bake uncovered 45 minutes. Distribute the olives over the top and blanket with the cheese. Bake 15 to 20 minutes or until the cheese is melted.

SERVES 8

ROWENA'S KIELBASA WITH CABBAGE AND APPLES

Rowena Morrel, who publishes the monthly magazine *In the Kitchen*, has been serving this easy, delicious dish to friends and family for many years.

1 pound kielbasa sausage, cut into 3-inch pieces
3/4 cup water, divided
1 1/4 pounds cabbage, thinly sliced
1 large tart green apple, peeled and thinly sliced
1 medium onion, peeled, chopped
2 tablespoons red wine vinegar or balsamic vinegar
2 tablespoons brown sugar
1/4 teaspoon salt
1/8 teaspoon black pepper
1 teaspoon caraway seeds

1. Preheat the oven to 375°F.

2. Puncture each kielbasa piece in several places with a fork. Poach it with 1/2 cup water in a 10-inch covered skillet until the water evaporates. Lightly brown the kielbasa. Transfer it to paper towels; pat off fat using paper towels. Pour off the fat in the skillet, reserving 2 tablespoons. Heat to medium.

3. Peel and slice the cabbage, apple, and onion. Add to the fat and cook 2 minutes while stirring.

4. Combine remaining 1/4 cup water, vinegar, sugar, salt, pepper, and caraway seeds. Sprinkle the mixture over the cabbage mixture. Transfer to a 3-quart casserole. Place the kielbasa on top of the cabbage mixture, cover, and bake 25 to 30 minutes or until the cabbage is tender and the kielbasa is plump. Remove the cover and continue to cook while shaking the pan occasionally until some of the juices evaporate.

5. Serve with crusty rye bread and grainy mustard.

SERVES 4

SLOW COOKER CORNED BEEF AND CABBAGE

St. Patty's Day may come only once a year, but an Irish-style combination dinner is always welcome at potlucks. It's a versatile meal, delicious hot but also wonderful in sandwiches or in a Reuben casserole.

1 3 to 4 pound corned beef brisket
4 medium potatoes, peeled and halved
1 envelope dry onion soup mix
1 clove garlic, sliced
water
1 bay leaf
1 medium head green cabbage, cut in wedges

1. Rinse off the meat and pat dry with white paper towels. Discard any brine from the package.

2. Place the potatoes in the bottom of a slow cooker. Put the meat on top. Sprinkle with the onion soup mix and add the garlic. Pour enough water over the meat to cover. Place the bay leaf on the meat. Sprinkle in the seasoning packet that comes with the meat, if desired. Cover the cooker.

3. Cook at high 6 to 8 hours. Transfer the meat and potatoes to a platter, cover, and keep warm; remove the bay leaf.

4. Place the cabbage into the hot liquid. Cook on high 30 to 45 minutes or until it is cooked to your preference.

5. Beginning at a pointed end, slice the meat into thin pieces against the grain and arrange overlapping on a platter. Surround with the potatoes; place the cabbage in a separate bowl. Serve with various mustards, and add a cruet of vinegar for seasoning the cabbage.

SERVES 6 TO 8

TIP: Bring this to potlucks with loaves of Irish soda bread and enjoy good ale with it.

BEEF AND MACARONI CASSEROLE I

You can count on children eating every morsel of this wonderful all-American dish.

    2 tablespoons vegetable oil
    1 cup chopped onion
    2 pounds lean ground beef
    1/2 teaspoon salt
    1/2 teaspoon pepper
    1 14.5-ounce can stewed tomatoes
    1 15-ounce can tomato sauce
    1 cup water
    1/2 cup small elbow macaroni, uncooked
    2 tablespoons chopped parsley
    1 1/2 cups shredded cheddar cheese

1. Preheat the oven to 350°F. Lightly oil a 2 1/2-quart casserole and set aside.

2. Warm the oil in a large skillet and sauté the onion until soft. Add the meat, mixing it with the onion and cooking until it is no longer pink, breaking up the large pieces. Drain in a strainer to remove excess fat. Wipe the skillet with paper towels.

3. Return the meat to the skillet. Season the meat with salt and pepper. Add the stewed tomatoes, tomato sauce, water, macaroni, and parsley, stirring to combine. Bring to a boil.

4. Transfer the mixture to the prepared casserole and top with the cheese.

5. Bake 30 minutes or until the macaroni tests tender, the sauce is bubbly, and the cheese is melted and golden brown.

SERVES 4

TIP: Prepare this dish through step 4, cover, and refrigerate until needed.

BEEF AND MACARONI CASSEROLE II

This delicious variation of the basic dish contains colorful vegetables and a hint of Tex-Mex seasoning.

2 tablespoons vegetable oil
1 1/2 pounds extra-lean ground beef or chuck
1/2 cup chopped onion
1 1/2 cups small egg noodles
1 cup corn, frozen or canned, drained
1/2 cup frozen green peas
1 15-ounce can tomato sauce
1 cup water
1/2 cup mild salsa, or to taste
1/3 cup shredded cheddar cheese

1. Preheat the oven to 350°F. Lightly oil a 2 1/2-quart casserole and set aside.

2. Warm the oil in a large skillet and brown the meat with the onion until the meat is no longer pink, breaking up the large pieces. Drain in a strainer to remove excess fat. Wipe the skillet with paper towels.

3. Return the meat to the skillet. Stir in the noodles, corn, peas, tomato sauce, water, and salsa. Bring to a boil, reduce the heat to moderately low, cover, and cook about 15 minutes or until the noodles are tender. Transfer to the prepared casserole and top with the cheese.

4. Bake 20 minutes or until the ingredients are bubbly and the cheese is melted and golden brown.

SERVES 4 TO 6

MARGE'S WESTERN BEAN AND BEEF CASSEROLE

This tasty mix of ingredients is my friend's old reliable dish for casual potlucks.

1 envelope dry onion soup mix

1/3 cup boiling water

2 tablespoons vegetable oil

1 1/2 pounds lean ground beef or chuck

2 18-ounce jars baked beans

1 14.75-ounce can baked beans in tomato sauce

1 1-pound can red kidney beans, drained

1/4 cup light brown sugar

1 tablespoon white vinegar

1 tablespoon ketchup

1. Preheat the oven to 350°F. Lightly butter a 9 x 13-inch baking dish and set aside.

2. Dissolve the onion soup mix in the boiling water and set aside.

3. Warm the oil in a large skillet and brown the meat until no longer pink, breaking up the large pieces. Drain the meat of excess fat in a strainer. Wipe out the skillet with paper towels.

4. Return the meat to the skillet, add the onion soup, and combine with all the beans. Stir in the sugar, vinegar, and ketchup over moderately high heat and bring to a boil.

5. Transfer mixture into baking dish. Bake uncovered 30 to 40 minutes, until bubbly and thickened.

SERVES 8 TO 10

PAM'S WONDERFUL ENCHILADA PIE CASSEROLE

Sometimes Pam makes an enchilada pie with her Black Bean Chili con Carne, which she prepares a couple of days before a potluck fiesta.

2 dozen corn tortillas

Pam's Black Bean Chili con Carne (see page 46)

2 to 3 pounds shredded or grated sharp cheddar cheese

2 4-ounce cans diced chiles, drained

1 15 ounce can yellow corn, drained

2 green bell peppers, chopped

1 3 1/2-ounce can sliced black olives

1. Preheat the oven to 350°F. Lightly oil a 9 x 13-inch or 10 x 15-inch baking dish and set aside.

2. Arrange an overlapping layer of the tortillas on the bottom of the prepared casserole. Layer on the chili, cheese, chiles, corn, bell peppers, and olives. Continue layering the ingredients, making certain the tortillas overlap, until 2 inches remain open at the top. End with a layer of chili; cover with cheese. Pat down the cheese a bit.

3. Loosely cover the casserole with aluminum foil. Bake 35 to 45 minutes or until thoroughly heated, the sauce is bubbly, and the cheese is melted.

SERVES 8 TO 10

SLOW COOKER PORK ROAST WITH CRANBERRIES AND RED WINE SAUCE

This succulent pork roast lived in my dreams until I bought a slow cooker to create and test recipes for this book. I couldn't believe the remarkable results! The pork and sauce were virtually identical to the meal I remembered from many years ago, but had eluded me because I used traditional cooking methods. Bay leaves impart a subtle flavor to braised dishes. There are two kinds: the stronger California and the less obtrusive Turkish.

1 3-pound boneless pork loin
1 16-ounce can whole cranberry sauce
2 envelopes dry onion soup mix
1 cup merlot or cabernet sauvignon
2 tablespoons olive oil
2 tablespoons unsalted butter
1 bay leaf

1. Remove the netting on the pork loin. Score the fat in a crosshatch pattern.

2. Whisk together the cranberry sauce, onion soup mix, and wine in a measuring cup.

3. Warm the oil and butter in a large skillet over moderate heat. Add the pork loin and brown well on all sides. Place the pork in the slow cooker. Pour the wine mixture over the pork. Place the bay leaf on top of the pork.

4. Cover and cook on high 1 hour. Reduce the temperature to low and cook 7 to 8 hours or until the meat is fork-tender.

5. Remove the meat from the cooker and allow it to rest 10 minutes before slicing. Arrange slices on a platter drizzled with liquid from the cooker. Pass additional liquid in a gravy boat.

SERVES 10

TIP: For a richly flavored entrée, I urge you to brown the pork first before braising it in the aromatic liquid. It makes a big difference.

POULTRY ENTRÉES

Cooking with poultry is great fun. Like a blank canvas awaiting the artist's brush, poultry's straightforward texture and flavor opens up amazing creativity. Herbs, both dried and fresh, impart distinctive tastes and aromas; vegetables and grains add their own character and augment nutrition. Whether fried southern-style or cloaked in a crust and made into a pie, poultry makes delicious dishes. Turkey Pie wears a colorful topping of sweet potato biscuits; Chicken Country Captain braises in a blend of tomatoes seasoned with curry powder; Judy's Chicken Adobo, the national dish of the Philippines, stews chicken in soy sauce; and Natalie's Chicken with Ham in Wine Sauce balances salty ham with the richness of wine to create a triumphant play of flavors

THE EASIEST BAKED OREGANO CHICKEN WITH POTATOES CASSEROLE

When I was newly married, this was the only dish I knew how to prepare for potluck dinners, and I made it for years. People still remind me of the "great oregano chicken dish" they had forty-five years ago.

3 teaspoons dried oregano, or to taste

1 teaspoon salt

1/2 teaspoon black pepper

3 cloves garlic, minced

2 1/2 to 3 pounds bone-in chicken breast
  halves, with skin

olive oil

2 to 3 pounds potatoes, peeled and cut
  into quarters

1. Position a rack in the upper third of the oven; preheat the oven to 375°F. Lightly oil a 9 x 13-inch casserole and set aside.

2. Combine the oregano, salt, pepper, and garlic. Set aside.

3. Rub the chicken breasts with oil. Use half the oregano mixture to sprinkle over the chicken and to rub into the skin and exposed flesh. Place the chicken in the prepared casserole.

4. Place the potatoes in a large bowl. Sprinkle 3 tablespoons of oil and the remaining oregano mixture on the potatoes. Mix the potatoes with the oregano mixture using your hands. Place the potatoes around the chicken.

5. Bake 50 minutes or until the chicken is tender and the potatoes are cooked and brown around the edges. Serve from the casserole.

SERVES 6

TIP: If the chicken needs more browning, increase the temperature to 425°F and bake several more minutes.

DALIA'S DEEP-DISH CHICKEN PIE

This wonderful dish is a classic, American treat of chicken and vegetables in a creamy sauce topped with tender piecrust.

1/3 cup unsalted butter

1/3 cup chopped onion

1/3 cup all-purpose flour

1/2 teaspoon salt

1/4 teaspoon black pepper

1 1/2 cups chicken broth

2/3 cup half-and-half

2 1/2 to 3 cups cooked chicken breast, cut into bite-size pieces

3 carrots, cooked and diced

1 cup frozen peas, thawed

1 6-ounce jar sliced mushrooms, drained

1 2-crust 15-ounce box refrigerated piecrust

1. Preheat the oven to 425°F. Butter a 9-inch deep-dish pie plate and set aside.

2. Melt the butter in a medium saucepan. Add the onion and cook until soft. Stir in the flour, salt, and pepper until well blended.

3. Add the broth, then the half-and-half while stirring until well combined, bubbly, and thickened. Remove the pan from the heat and mix in the chicken, carrots, peas, and mushrooms.

4. Transfer the mixture to the prepared pie plate. Fit the piecrust over the filling, folding the edges under and crimping attractively. Make several slits in the top with the point of a paring knife.

5. Bake 30 to 40 minutes or until the crust is golden brown. Allow the pie to settle 5 minutes before serving.

SERVES 6

JUDY'S CHICKEN ADOBO

This aromatic chicken stew belongs to my daughter-in-law Judy's collection of heritage recipes. The marriage of soy sauce with white vinegar imparts seasoning and succulence to the chicken and provides plenty of tasty gravy for the rice side dish. Adobo is the national dish of the Philippines and is equally tasty when made with pork.

6 cloves garlic, smashed
1/2 tablespoon black peppercorns
5 whole bay leaves
1/4 cup soy sauce
1/2 cup white wine vinegar
1 teaspoon onion powder
1 3 to 4 pound chicken, cut into 8 pieces
4 cups cooked white rice

1. Combine all the ingredients except the chicken and rice in a Dutch oven. Bring the mixture to a full rolling boil. Add the chicken to the Dutch oven, reduce heat, cover, and cook 30 minutes. Turn the chicken over and cook covered 30 minutes or until fork-tender.

2. Preheat broiler. Line pan with aluminum foil.

3. Remove chicken from Dutch oven and place skin side up in the broiler pan. Broil until skin is crispy and brown — just a quick "run" under the broiler.

4. Meanwhile, boil the Dutch oven mixture uncovered until reduced by half. The oil from the chicken will combine with the soy sauce mixture and thicken, actually emulsify, into gravy.

5. Place the chicken on a serving platter and serve with mounds of white rice. Pass the gravy separately to ladle over the chicken and rice.

SERVES 6 TO 8

62

CICI'S KING RANCH CASSEROLE

This fantastic Texas recipe comes from my friend and colleague, CiCi Williamson, a Texan, food and travel writer, and author of *The Best of Virginia Farms Tour Book and Cookbook* as well as many microwave cookbooks. Trying to authenticate the history of this great dish seems impossible. Ann Criswell, CiCi's editor at the *Houston Chronicle* for more than thirty years, speculates the King family has never taken credit probably because a ranch cook concocted it for cowboys. The King Ranch, in Kingsville, Texas, is a national historic landmark and the largest ranch in the world. CiCi contends Texans begin eating this casserole early in their lives. "Any time I've taken it to a potluck, you're out of luck if you don't get some early because the casserole is always scraped clean. And never use flour tortillas; it must have the flavor of corn tortillas."

1 10 3/4-ounce can condensed cream of mushroom soup
1 10 3/4-ounce can condensed cream of chicken soup
1 10-ounce can tomatoes with green chiles, including liquid
1/2 cup chicken broth
12 6-inch corn tortillas, torn into 1-inch pieces
1 3 to 4 pound chicken, cut into pieces and poached, or 4 cups leftover cooked chicken or turkey, cut into bite-size pieces
2 medium onions, finely chopped
3 cups shredded sharp cheddar cheese

1. Preheat the oven to 350°F. Butter a 3-quart rectangular casserole and set aside.

2. Combine the chicken soup, mushroom soup, tomatoes, and the broth; set aside.

3. Begin layering one-third of the ingredients in the prepared casserole in the following order: corn tortilla pieces, chicken, soup mixture, chopped onion, and cheese. Repeat, making two more layers, ending with the cheese.

4. Bake 45 minutes or until the cheese browns and the dish is bubbly hot.

SERVES 8 (6 IF FEEDING TEXANS!)

TIPS: If you're in a hurry, assemble the casserole in a glass dish that fits into your microwave. Heat on high 11 to 13 minutes. It's also possible to obtain tasty, quick results using corn chips instead of corn tortillas. For a milder onion flavor, briefly sauté the chopped onions in a little butter before adding them to the casserole. It makes a big difference.

SOUTHERN FRIED CHICKEN

I learned how to make this exceptional version of fried chicken from Miss Anna Cobbs, a stately black woman who helped take care of my four sons. What did I, a former resident of Yankee-land, know about this Southern specialty? Miss Anna said I must cover the skillet when the chicken is frying, the only fried dish she knew of using this technique. Then the chicken goes into the oven, "keepin' warm and crispin' up." Note that the chicken must rest 2 to 3 1/2 hours before frying.

1 3 1/2-pound package chicken parts,
    cut into 8 pieces
water
2 small soft lemons, halved
1 teaspoon salt
1/2 teaspoon black pepper
1/2 to 3/4 cup self-rising flour
1 teaspoon sweet paprika
vegetable shortening for frying
Cream Gravy (optional; see recipe page 65)

1. Trim the chicken pieces of fat flaps and rinse in cold running water. Place in a large bowl, cover with cold water, and squeeze the juice from the lemons into the water. Allow the chickens to soak at least 2 to 3 hours in the refrigerator. Drain and dry the chicken well with paper towels.

2. Mix the salt and pepper and season the chicken. Allow the chicken to sit about 30 minutes.

3. Place the flour and paprika in a paper bag. Shake each piece of chicken in the bag to coat evenly.

4. Melt 1 cup of the shortening in a large heavy skillet (cast iron is best) over moderately high heat until it is hot. (Test by placing a cube of plain white bread in the oil. If the bread browns in 30 seconds, the oil is ready.)

5. Preheat the oven to 300°F.

6. Add the chicken to the shortening a few pieces at a time, skin side down. Cover the skillet and fry 8 to 10 minutes. Turn the pieces over, cover, and fry 8 to 10 minutes longer. Uncover the pan, lower the heat, and fry 5 minutes. Drain the chicken on paper towels, reserving brown crumbles from the pan if making gravy. Put the chicken pieces on a baking sheet and place in the oven with the door slightly ajar. Fry the remaining chicken pieces as above, melting more shortening as necessary.

7. Serve the chicken hot and crisp from the oven. Pass the Cream Gravy, if using, separately.

SERVES 4 TO 6

CREAM GRAVY

1/2 cup light cream
1/2 cup whole milk
2 tablespoons instant flour

1. Combine cream and milk. Whisk in the flour until smooth.

2. After frying the meat, drain all the fat from the skillet, but leave the brown crumbles sticking to the bottom. Pour in the cream mixture while stirring with a wooden spoon, scraping to release the crumbles. Bring the mixture to a boil over moderately high heat, lower the heat, and cook gently 1 minute or more, until thickened.

MAKES 1 CUP

CREAMY HERB CHICKEN AND BROCCOLI CASSEROLE

This is a nice, easy casserole combining chicken and broccoli with a smooth cheese-enriched sauce. Turkey makes a perfect alternative to chicken.

2 teaspoons Italian seasoning
1/4 teaspoon salt
pinch black pepper
1/2 teaspoon sweet paprika
1 pound chicken breasts, boned and skinned
1 cup evaporated milk or half-and-half, divided
2 tablespoons all-purpose flour
1 clove garlic, finely minced
3/4 to 1 cup shredded gruyère or swiss cheese, divided
1/4 cup grated Parmesan cheese
2 10-ounce packages frozen broccoli florets or cuts, thawed, rinsed, and drained
2 to 3 tablespoons unsalted butter

1. Preheat the oven to 350°F. Butter a 2 1/2-quart casserole and set aside.

2. Combine Italian seasoning, salt, pepper, and paprika. Place chicken breast on wax paper and lightly sprinkle seasoning mix on both sides, saving a bit for the cheese sauce. Cover the chicken with another piece of wax paper and gently pound to even thinness. Slice into bite-size pieces or slender strips.

CONTINUED >

3. Whisk 1/4 cup evaporated milk into the flour in a small saucepan. Whisk in the remaining 3/4 cup evaporated milk; add the garlic and any remaining seasoning from step 1 that did not touch the raw chicken. Cook the mixture over moderate heat while stirring until the mixture thickens and comes to a boil. Remove the pan from the heat. Stir in the gruyère cheese, reserving 4 tablespoons.

4. Combine the remaining 4 tablespoons gruyère cheese with the Parmesan cheese. Set aside.

5. Pour 1/3 cup of the cheese sauce on the bottom of the prepared casserole, tilting to distribute it evenly. Place the broccoli over the sauce.

6. Melt the butter over moderate heat in a large skillet and sauté the chicken, tossing the pieces until lightly brown. Arrange the pieces over the broccoli as they are cooked.

7. Pour the remaining cheese sauce over the chicken. Sprinkle with the remaining cheese mixture. Bake 30 minutes or until the cheese melts and the topping is golden brown. Allow the casserole to settle 5 minutes before serving.

SERVES 6

TURKEY PIE WITH SWEET POTATO BISCUITS

Prepare this tasty dish any time of the year; it's a natural during the holidays, when these ingredients fit the season.

3 chicken bouillon cubes
2 cups boiling water
4 tablespoons unsalted butter
1 tablespoon dehydrated minced onion
1/2 teaspoon garlic salt
1/2 teaspoon sweet paprika
pinch black pepper
4 tablespoons all-purpose flour
3 cups cooked turkey, cut into bite-size pieces
2 to 3 cups frozen mixed vegetables of choice
1 tablespoon minced parsley leaves
Sweet Potato Biscuits (see recipe page 67)
melted butter (optional)

1. Preheat the oven to 400°F. Lightly butter a 9 x 13-inch casserole and set aside.

2. Dissolve bouillon cubes in the water and set aside.

3. Melt the butter in a skillet over moderate heat. Stir in the onion, garlic salt, paprika, and pepper. Cook while stirring until the onion softens. Add the flour and stir to blend. Add the bouillon and stir until the sauce thickens and bubbles. Stir in the turkey and vegetables and cook until the mixture is hot and begins bubbling. Remove the pan from the heat and stir in the parsley. Transfer the mixture to the prepared casserole.

4. Place the biscuits on the turkey mixture, leaving space between each one. Brush with a little melted butter, if using. (Bake extra biscuits on a separate baking sheet.)

5. Bake 15 minutes or until the ingredients are hot and bubbly and the biscuits are lightly browned.

SERVES 4 TO 6

SWEET POTATO BISCUITS

1 cup all-purpose flour
3 teaspoons baking powder
2 teaspoons sugar
1/2 teaspoon salt
1/3 cup vegetable shortening
1 cup mashed or puréed sweet potatoes
3 to 4 tablespoons milk

1. Combine the flour, baking powder, sugar, and salt in a large bowl. Cut the shortening into the dry ingredients until the mixture resembles tiny peas. Mix in the sweet potatoes.

2. Add 3 tablespoons of milk to the dry ingredients. Mix the ingredients with a fork until a soft dough forms and cleans the bowl. Add the remaining tablespoon of milk if dough is dry and doesn't form a neat ball.

3. Toss the dough onto a lightly floured surface and knead several times for smoothness. Sprinkle the work surface, dough, and rolling pin with a light dusting of flour and roll the dough to 1/2-inch thickness. Cut out biscuits using a 2 1/2- to 3-inch cutter.

MAKES ABOUT 12 BISCUITS

CAPTAIN'S COUNTRY CHICKEN

James Beard, the father of American gastronomy, ranks this dish second only to Southern Fried Chicken in our culinary heritage. Historians think versions of this exceptional combination have been prepared in our country since colonial days. Another possibility suggests a British captain sailed into Savannah Harbor early in our country's history, and because guests were coming for dinner he used what he had on hand to put together a meal. I am grateful to Cecily Brownstone of the Associated Press for researching this recipe in the 1950s and recreating the dish based on this and other historical information.

8 to 10 assorted chicken pieces, trimmed of
    excess skin and fat flaps
1/3 cup all-purpose flour
1 teaspoon salt
1/2 teaspoon sweet paprika
1/4 teaspoon black pepper
3 tablespoons unsalted butter
1 tablespoon vegetable oil
1/3 cup finely chopped onion
1/3 cup finely diced green pepper
1 clove garlic, minced
1 1/2 to 2 teaspoons curry powder
1/2 teaspoon dried thyme

2 1-pound cans stewed tomatoes
3 tablespoons currants
cooked white rice
toasted slivered almonds (optional)

1. Rinse and dry the chicken pieces. Combine the flour, salt, paprika, and pepper on wax paper. Coat the chicken with the mixture, shake off the excess, and set the pieces aside.

2. Melt the butter with the oil in a large skillet over moderate heat. Brown the chicken pieces on all sides. Place them, skin side up, in a 9 x 13-inch casserole.

3. Preheat the oven to 350°F.

4. Reserve 2 tablespoons of drippings from the skillet and discard the rest. Add the onion, green pepper, garlic, curry powder, and thyme to the skillet. Stir and cook over moderately low heat until the onion and green pepper are softened and the brown bits from the bottom of the skillet are loosened. Add the stewed tomatoes, crushing them with a potato masher, and bring to a boil.

5. Pour the mixture over the chicken and stir in the currants. Cover and bake 50 minutes to 1 hour or until the chicken is fork-tender. (If the sauce looks dry, reduce the oven temperature to 325°F.) Uncover the casserole and bake 10 to 15 minutes. Serve on a large platter atop a mound of white rice; sprinkle with almonds, if using.

TIPS: I use quartered bone-in chicken breasts and boneless chicken thighs instead of cut-up chicken. Curry powder comes in three degrees of heat: mild, medium, and hot. I season this dish with mild curry powder because of its spunky flavor.

CRISPY OVEN-FRIED CHICKEN

Less labor intensive than skillet-fried chicken, this method calls for floured and breaded chicken parts to bake at a high temperature. Note that the chicken must marinate at least 3 hours before baking.

> 3 to 4 pounds chicken parts, cut into 8 pieces,
>   trimmed of fat flaps
> buttermilk
> 8 tablespoons unsalted butter, divided
> 1/2 cup all-purpose flour
> 3/4 cup unseasoned dry bread crumbs
> 1/2 teaspoon salt
> 1/2 teaspoon sweet paprika
> pinch black pepper
> 1 tablespoon vegetable oil

1. Rinse the chicken in cool running water, shaking to eliminate excess water. Place the chicken in a large bowl and cover with buttermilk. Cover and refrigerate at least 3 hours.

2. Position the rack in the upper third of the oven. Preheat the oven to 425°F.

3. Melt 3 tablespoons of the butter in a small bowl and set aside.

4. Combine the flour, bread crumbs, salt, paprika, and pepper on wax paper.

5. Pat the chicken dry with white paper towels. Brush with a good coating of melted butter. Roll the chicken in the flour mixture and set aside.

6. Place a broiler pan or shallow baking pan with sides in the oven and melt the remaining 5 tablespoons of butter with the oil. Spread evenly over the pan. Place the chicken pieces in the butter, skin side down. Bake 30 minutes.

7. Turn the chicken over and bake 20 to 30 minutes or until crispy and golden brown and the juices run clear when pierced with a fork.

NATALIE'S CHICKEN WITH HAM IN WINE SAUCE

My daughter, Natalie, is a great intuitive cook. This is one of the dishes she "just does."

4 whole boneless chicken breasts, trimmed of fat flaps

1 individual-size Virginia ham steak

2 cups plus 1 tablespoon all-purpose flour, divided

dash salt and black pepper

olive oil

2 to 3 cups dry white wine

1/4 cup chicken broth

2 tablespoons chopped parsley

2 cups cooked white, brown, or wild rice blend

1. Rinse chicken breasts and wipe with paper towels. Place them between sheets of plastic wrap and lightly pound to an even thinness. Slice breast into thirds.

2. Slice the ham into sliver-size pieces.

3. Spread 2 cups of the flour on wax paper and combine with the salt and pepper. Dredge the chicken pieces in the flour, lightly coating on all sides.

4. Warm enough oil in a large skillet over moderately high heat to cover the bottom of the pan. Brown the chicken pieces on both sides and transfer to a platter. Cover with foil or wax paper.

5. Increase the heat to high, adding a little more oil, if necessary, and sauté the ham quickly, turning it over with a spatula to prevent burning. Remove the ham when the edges are lightly brown. Transfer to a separate plate and cover.

6. Pour the wine into the skillet and scrape up the crumbles left on the bottom. When the wine comes to a boil, transfer the chicken to the pan first, then the ham. Return the wine to a boil. Lower the heat to a simmer, cover, and simmer 20 minutes or until the chicken tests done.

7. Lift the chicken from the skillet with a slotted spoon and transfer it to a warm serving casserole.

8. To make the sauce, whisk the remaining 1 tablespoon of flour into the broth, stirring until smooth. Stir into the bubbling wine in the skillet. Bring to a boil while stirring, reduce the heat, and simmer a few minutes until the sauce thickens. Stir in the parsley. Pour over the chicken in the casserole. Serve with rice, if desired.

SERVES 8

TIPS: This dish goes with every vegetable accompaniment imaginable. Sometimes Natalie adds a pound of sautéed sliced mushrooms to the sauce and changes the personality by using Marsala, the fortified sweet Sicilian wine, instead of dry white wine.

JANE'S CHICKEN AND VEGETABLES WITH BARBECUE SAUCE

Jane Meganhauser, a colleague, shared this recipe she picked up at the National Chicken Cooking Contest many years ago. Although it wasn't a prize winner, Jane revised the original recipe, prepared it "a thousand times," and has given it to everyone she knows.

Barbecue sauce:

2 tablespoons vegetable oil

1/2 cup chopped onion

1/2 cup ketchup

1/4 cup water

2 tablespoons sugar

2 tablespoons apple cider vinegar

1 tablespoon Worcestershire sauce

1 scant tablespoon prepared mustard

1/2 teaspoon black pepper

Chicken and vegetables:

8 to 10 assorted chicken pieces, trimmed of
    excess skin and fat flaps

6 potatoes, peeled and quartered

6 sweet onions, peeled and quartered

1. Preheat oven to 400°F. Oil 9 x 13-inch baking dish.

2. To make the barbecue sauce, warm the oil in a saucepan and sauté the onion until softened. Add the remaining ingredients and combine thoroughly. Cook over moderately low heat 15 to 20 minutes while stirring occasionally. Remove the pan from the heat and set aside.

3. Place the chicken in a single layer in the prepared casserole or in two pans. Place the vegetables in between the chicken pieces. Pour the barbecue sauce over all the ingredients. Cover with aluminum foil and bake 30 to 40 minutes, basting once or twice.

4. Remove the foil and cook 15 to 20 minutes or until chicken juices run clear and the chicken and vegetables are fork-tender. For a more golden-brown chicken skin, place the casserole under the broiler a few minutes or increase the oven temperature to 450°F and bake several minutes.

SERVES 6 TO 8

TIPS: This recipe doubles and triples easily. Jane often makes quantities of sauce and freezes it. She recommends not using bottled barbecue sauce because it is too potent, and she suggests using broiler-fryer quarters instead of chicken parts. She often covers and refrigerates the casserole the night before or in the morning and takes it out while the oven is preheating. Cooking time varies with the sizes of the chicken pieces and whether the dish is still cold.

JUDITH FERTIG'S CHURCH SUPPER CHICKEN AND WILD RICE HOT DISH

Judith likes to make this dish during the cold months, especially after Thanksgiving when there's an abundance of turkey to use in place of chicken.

2 boxes wild rice mix

4 tablespoons unsalted butter

1/2 cup chopped onion

4 tablespoons all-purpose flour

1 1/2 cups chicken broth

1 1/2 cups half-and-half

salt and black pepper to taste

1/4 teaspoon ground nutmeg

1 4-ounce jar sliced mushrooms, drained

3 cups cooked, diced chicken

2 tablespoons chopped fresh parsley

1 cup grated brick, Muenster, or other mild
   white cheese

1. Preheat the oven to 350°F. Butter an oval 2 1/2-quart or 9 x 13-inch casserole and set aside.

2. Cook the wild rice according to package directions. Set aside.

3. Melt the butter over moderate heat. Add the onion and sauté until it softens but does not brown. Sprinkle in the flour and stir to blend. Pour in the broth and half-and-half; whisk until the sauce is smooth. Simmer 5 minutes. Add the salt, pepper, and nutmeg. Add the mushrooms, chicken, parsley, and cooked wild rice to the sauce; thoroughly combine.

4. Transfer the mixture into the prepared casserole. Sprinkle the cheese over the top. Bake 30 minutes or until hot and bubbling and the cheese is golden brown.

SERVES 8 TO 10

VEGETABLE SIDE DISHES AND SALADS

egetable dishes bring vibrant colors as well as exceptional flavors, fiber, and nutrition to the potluck. These casseroles round out the meal and balance both rich and simple entrées. Most are ready to pop in the oven at a moment's notice. Consider Baby Brussels Sprouts with Brown Rice, Carrot and Parmesan Cheese Casserole, and Elizabeth's Paprika Potato Stew for unusual, delicious offerings. Some salads are great cold, such as Perfection Salad and Murphy's Grand Potato Salad; others, such as Sheilah's Elegant Rice Salad and Ken Haedrich's Wheat Bread and Tomato Salad, are tastier at room temperature. Many vegetable casseroles hold a meal together. Their versatility as side dishes or as stand-alone entrées gives them the capacity to become everyone's favorite part of the meal.

Many vegetable casseroles require two steps: a partial cooking followed by putting the dish together. Often the microwave provides invaluable, quick service for the cooking phase.

PAM'S LETHALLY FATTENING POTATO CASSEROLE

Pam Palmer, a food-loving colleague, sent me this recipe, saying, "Don't be tempted to use any low-fat ingredients (or margarine) because it just won't taste as good." As part of a potluck dinner, a little goes a long way.

2 cups sour cream
1 10 3/4-ounce can cream of chicken soup
2 pounds frozen small tater tots, thawed
3/4 cup unsalted butter, melted and divided
1/2 cup onion, chopped
2 cups grated cheddar cheese
2 cups crushed cornflakes

1. Preheat the oven to 350°F. Lightly butter a 2 1/2-quart or 9 x 13-inch casserole and set aside.

2. Mix the sour cream and soup together in a large bowl. Add the potatoes with 1/2 cup butter, onion, and cheese; combine thoroughly. Transfer to the prepared casserole.

3. Bake 30 minutes. Mix the remaining 1/4 cup butter with the cornflakes and distribute on top of the mixture, pressing down lightly.

4. Bake 15 to 20 minutes or until the mixture is bubbling and a light golden brown. Watch the cornflakes so they do not burn.

SERVES 10 TO 12

MURPHY FAMILY'S GRAND POTATO SALAD

Exceptional potato salads are rare, but here is one outstanding recipe, a specialty of the Murphy family, friends from the Philadelphia area. Resist substituting mayonnaise for the salad dressing because it is just not the same. Note that the salad must be refrigerated overnight before serving.

5 pounds red potatoes
1 32-ounce jar salad dressing, divided
3 large hard-cooked eggs, chopped
1 teaspoon salt
1/2 teaspoon black pepper
1 tablespoon yellow mustard
1 teaspoon white vinegar
1 to 2 tablespoons milk
2 teaspoons sugar
3 cups chopped celery
1 small onion, finely minced
paprika, for garnish
1 hard-cooked egg, sliced, for garnish
fresh parsley sprigs, for garnish

1. Boil the potatoes in plenty of water until easily pierced with a fork. (Doneness varies according to the potato sizes.) Drain well. Peel the potatoes while warm and cut into medium dice. Mix the salad dressing with the eggs, salt, pepper, mustard, vinegar, milk, and sugar until thoroughly combined.

2. Place the potatoes in a large bowl. Add the celery, onion, and 3/4 of the salad dressing mixture. Gently fold the ingredients together. Test for seasoning, adding salt and pepper as necessary.

3. Cover the potato salad and refrigerate overnight.

4. When ready to serve, add the remaining 8 ounces of the salad dressing and combine thoroughly.

5. Transfer the salad to a large serving bowl. Garnish the top with a light dusting of paprika, the sliced eggs, and tiny bouquets of parsley sprigs.

SERVES AT LEAST 12

TIPS: The salad is tastier when the dressing is added to warm potatoes. The easiest way to chop hard-cooked eggs is to place them in an egg slicer in one direction, then in the opposite way. To make hard-cooked eggs, see the recipe for Deviled Eggs on page 19.

MARGE HUBBARD'S SWEET POTATO CASSEROLE

This is Marge's specialty casserole; it's always a part of her holiday dinners. Friends have tried a shortcut by substituting sugar-coated flakes for the unsweetened ones, but it's just not the same.

2 1-pound 1-ounce cans sweet potatoes, drained
 and liquid reserved
1 20-ounce can crushed pineapple with juice
1/8 teaspoon ground nutmeg
1/2 teaspoon salt
2 tablespoons plus 1/3 cup packed light
 brown sugar, divided
4 tablespoons unsalted butter
1/2 cup (1 stick) unsalted butter, melted
2 cups cornflakes

1. Preheat the oven to 325°F. Butter a 2-quart casserole and set aside.

2. Mash the sweet potatoes; add the pineapple, nutmeg, salt, 2 tablespoons sugar, and 4 tablespoons butter. Mix in the reserved sweet potato liquid to make a soft consistency. Transfer the mixture to the prepared casserole.

3. To make the topping, combine the remaining 1/3 cup sugar and the melted butter. Add the cornflakes and toss until well coated. Distribute evenly over the sweet potato mixture.

4. Bake uncovered 40 minutes or until golden brown.

SERVES 8 TO 10

ELIZABETH'S PAPRIKA POTATO STEW

My mother-in-law, a foremost cook, came from Old Hungary. Although she cooked dishes from all cuisines, she was partial to Hungarian preparations. The Turks brought paprika in the form of sweet peppers to Hungary during their fifteenth-century invasions, which the Hungarians made into a spice that set the world standard for paprika.

3 tablespoons vegetable oil or unsalted butter
1 large onion, finely chopped
2 tablespoons sweet Hungarian paprika
2 1/2 pounds firm new boiling potatoes, peeled,
 halved, and cut into 1/4-inch slices
1 teaspoon salt
water

1. Warm the oil in a large saucepan suitable for a table presentation; sauté the onion until soft. Mix in the paprika and stir over moderately low heat, cooking gently a few minutes.

2. Add the potatoes, tossing them so they are well coated with the paprika. Sprinkle with salt, gradually add enough water to just reach the top of the potatoes, cover, and simmer 20 to 25 minutes or until they can be pierced easily with a fork.

3. Uncover and allow the mixture to bubble a few minutes. Serve piping hot.

SERVES 6 TO 8

SMOTHERED CABBAGE CASSEROLE

This tasty side dish rounds out a meal nicely. My husband loves cabbage, particularly the crinkly leafed Savoy, which I use when it is available during the cooler months of the year.

    4 tablespoons vegetable oil
    1 medium yellow onion, chopped
    1 medium to large potato, peeled and chopped
    1 head (about 2 pounds) Savoy or other
        cabbage, thinly sliced
    4 plump carrots, trimmed, peeled, and cut
        into 1-inch lengths
    1 10 3/4-ounce can condensed cream of celery soup
    3/4 cup chicken or vegetable broth

1. Preheat the oven to 350°F. Lightly butter a 2 1/2- or 3-quart casserole with a cover and set aside.

2. Warm the oil with the onion and potato over medium heat in a large skillet until the onion softens. Stir in the cabbage and carrots until well mixed. Combine the soup and broth. Stir into the cabbage mixture and bring to a boil.

3. Transfer to the prepared casserole and cover. Bake 30 minutes. Remove the cover and bake 20 minutes or until the mixture is blended and deliciously tender.

SERVES 4 TO 6

TIP: To chop vegetables effortlessly, use a food processor and pulse the large pieces.

BABY BRUSSELS SPROUTS WITH BROWN RICE CASSEROLE

This dish came about during a holiday season marathon of meals when I decided I had to give leftovers a makeover. If specially cultivated tiny Brussels sprouts aren't available in your area, use the regular size and cut them in half.

> 1 20-ounce bag frozen tiny Brussels sprouts
> 1/3 cup boiling water
> 4 tablespoons unsalted butter
> 4 scallions, trimmed and thinly sliced
> 3 tablespoons all-purpose flour
> 1 1/4 cups chicken broth
> 1 1/4 cups milk
> 1/4 teaspoon salt
> pinch black pepper
> 1 cup cooked brown rice
> 3 tablespoons grated Parmesan cheese
> 1/3 cup dry unseasoned bread crumbs

1. Preheat the oven to 375°F. Lightly butter a 2 1/2- or 3-quart casserole and set aside.

2. Partially cook the Brussels sprouts in the water in a covered saucepan 5 minutes. Uncover and simmer 1 minute. Drain in a colander while shaking the colander. Rinse and dry the saucepan.

3. Melt the butter in the same saucepan over moderately low heat. Add the scallions and cook until limp. Whisk in the flour and cook while stirring until smooth. Pour in the broth and milk, raise the heat, and bring to a boil. Cook the sauce until bubbly and thick. Season with salt and pepper.

4. Distribute the rice on the bottom of the casserole. Place the Brussels sprouts, stems side down (or cut-side down, if halved), evenly over the rice. Pour the sauce over the Brussels sprouts. Sprinkle with the cheese and top with the bread crumbs.

5. Bake 25 to 30 minutes or until the ingredients are heated and the top is golden brown.

SERVES 5 TO 6

TALK-OF-THE-TOWN POTATO CASSEROLE

This is one of the greatest, easiest recipes ever devised. My grandchildren help me prepare this, and it always comes out right.

1/2 cup thinly sliced scallions

2 cups sour cream

1 10 3/4-ounce can cream of chicken soup

1 10 3/4-ounce can cream of celery soup

1 cup shredded cheddar cheese

black pepper, to taste

2 cups frozen small peas

1/2 cup chopped fresh parsley leaves

1 2-pound package frozen hash browns, slightly thawed

4 tablespoons (1/2 stick) unsalted butter, melted

1/4 to 1/3 cup unseasoned dry bread crumbs

1. Preheat the oven to 350°F. Lightly butter a 9 x 13-inch casserole and set aside.

2. Combine the scallions, sour cream, both soups, cheese, pepper, peas, and parsley in a large bowl. Gently fold in the hash browns. Transfer the mixture to the prepared casserole.

3. Combine the butter with the bread crumbs in a small bowl. Sprinkle the crumbs evenly over the top of the potato mixture.

4. Bake 45 minutes to 1 hour or until nicely browned.

SERVES 10 TO 12

TIP: You can prepare this dish early and refrigerate it. Add 15 minutes to the baking time if it is cold when you put it in the oven.

STEWED RED CABBAGE CASSEROLE

I've been preparing red cabbage in this style for almost forty-five years. A nicely balanced dish, it usually turns out purple, which, I understand from a German friend, is the way it is supposed to be.

6 slices bacon, diced

1 tablespoon vegetable oil

1 tablespoon sugar

1 large onion, diced

1 tart apple, peeled and grated

2 1/2 to 3-pounds red cabbage, cored, quartered, and sliced

1/4 cup red wine vinegar, heated

2 or more cups chicken or vegetable broth, heated

1. In a heavy casserole or Dutch oven suitable for table presentation, cook the bacon in the oil over moderately high heat until it begins to give up its fat. Add the sugar, reduce the heat to moderately low, and continue sautéing the bacon until brown. Add the onion and apple into the fat; sauté slowly several minutes until the onion is limp and the apple is softened. Preheat the oven to 275°F.

2. Add the cabbage to the bacon mixture and toss so it glistens with the bacon fat. Pour the vinegar over the cabbage. Toss the cabbage so it mixes with the vinegar. Cover and braise over low heat 5 to 10 minutes. Uncover to see that the cabbage has changed from red to bright purple because of the acid (vinegar) ingredient. Add the broth and bring to a boil.

3. Cover the casserole and place in the oven. Braise about 2 hours or until cooked through. Check from time to time to see if it requires more hot broth. This dish does not have a sauce, but it requires liquid for braising. Serve piping hot from the casserole.

SERVES 6 TO 8

SHEILAH'S ELEGANT RICE SALAD

This rice salad comes from colleague Sheilah Kaufman's book, *Simply Irresistible: Easy, Elegant, Fearless, Fussless Cooking*. Rice-a-Roni, the foundation of this dish, hit the supermarket shelves in 1953 and debuted with a catchy jingle designating it as "the San Francisco treat." Note that the salad is refrigerated 4 to 8 hours before serving.

2 6-ounce packages chicken-flavored rice and vermicelli
    (such as Rice-a-Roni)
2 4-ounce jars marinated artichoke hearts
1/2 cup pitted black olives, sliced
6 scallions, sliced
1/2 cup whole egg mayonnaise
black pepper, to taste
1/2 cup diced pimentos

1. Prepare the rice according to the package directions. Allow the rice to cool to room temperature.

2. Drain the liquid from the artichoke hearts into a large bowl. Coarsely chop the artichoke hearts and add them to the liquid. Stir in the olives, scallions, mayonnaise, pepper, and pimentos. Stir in the cool rice, tossing to mix well.

3. Cover and refrigerate 4 to 8 hours before serving.

SERVES 12

CARROT AND PARMESAN CHEESE CASSEROLE

I prepared this combination a few Thanksgivings ago because we needed another side dish.

dry unseasoned bread crumbs for dusting,
    plus 2 tablespoons
1 pound carrots, scraped, trimmed,
    and cut into pieces
1/2 cup unsalted butter, melted
2 to 4 tablespoons heavy cream, divided
3/4 cup Parmesan cheese, divided
2 large eggs, beaten
2 tablespoons minced parsley
1/4 teaspoon salt
1/4 teaspoon black pepper

1. Preheat the oven to 350°F. Butter a 1 1/2-quart casserole or quiche dish and dust with the bread crumbs; set aside.

2. Cook the carrots in boiling salted water until fork tender.

3. Transfer the carrots to a blender or food processor. With the machine running, stream in the butter, 2 tablespoons heavy cream, 1/2 cup Parmesan cheese, and the eggs. Process until smooth. Pulse to fold in the parsley, salt, and pepper.

4. Transfer the mixture to the prepared casserole, smoothing the top. Sprinkle with the remaining 2 tablespoons bread crumbs and the remaining 1/4 cup Parmesan cheese.

5. Bake 35 to 45 minutes or until the casserole is puffed and the top is light golden brown. Serve piping hot from the oven.

SERVES 6 TO 8

TIP: You can prepare this dish early and refrigerate it. Add at least 10 minutes to the baking time if it is cold when you put it into the oven.

DALIA'S HOT CHICKEN SALAD

When you can't think of what to make, this is your dish. This super-easy combination goes together quickly and is great for a large group. Accompany it with vinaigrette-dressed sliced tomatoes.

1 cup whole egg mayonnaise

1/2 cup sour cream (optional)

1 10 3/4-ounce can cream of chicken soup

1 2-ounce jar pimentos, well drained

2 tablespoons lemon juice

1 tablespoon grated onion

4 cups cooked chicken, cut into bite-size pieces

3 cups thinly sliced celery

1 cup slivered almonds (optional)

1 cup grated sharp cheddar cheese

1 cup crushed potato chips (optional)

1. Preheat the oven to 400°F. Butter a 9 x 13-inch or 3-quart baking dish and set aside.

2. Combine the mayonnaise, sour cream, if using, soup, pimentos, lemon juice, and onion in a large bowl. Blend in the chicken, celery, and almonds, if using; mix lightly. Transfer to the prepared baking dish. Sprinkle with the cheese and the potato chips, if using.

3. Bake 25 minutes or until the ingredients are bubbly and the topping is golden brown. Serve piping hot.

SERVES 8

TIPS: Use a rotisserie chicken or turkey from the supermarket to make preparation a cinch. Prepare this dish ahead of time, cover, refrigerate, and relax before company arrives. Add 10 to 15 minutes baking time to the chilled dish.

KEN HAEDRICH'S WHEAT BREAD AND TOMATO SALAD

Says Ken Haedrich, author of *Pie: 300 Tried and True Recipes for Homemade Pie*: "Frugal cook that I am, I love the premise of giving slightly old bread new life by mixing it with juicy vegetables, olive oil, vinegar, and herbs. . . . The key here is not to moisten the bread too much. . . . Let the vegetable juices and dressing soak into the bread first. Then, and only then, do you add water to moisten the bread. Your choice of bread is important. Only use a firm country sourdough. Use a soft, cheap faux wheat bread and it will quickly turn into little wet cotton balls."

1/2 pound slightly dry whole wheat bread

3 good-size cucumbers

1 large red bell pepper, finely diced

1 small zucchini, finely diced

1 small red onion, halved and thinly sliced

2 to 3 pounds small, ripe tomatoes

1 cup good-quality olives, halved and pitted

1/4 teaspoon salt, plus more to taste

1/3 cup olive oil

2 tablespoons red wine vinegar

1 clove garlic, minced

2 to 3 tablespoons chopped fresh parsley

2 to 3 tablespoons chopped fresh basil leaves

black pepper, to taste

1. Trim the crusts from the bread and cut the bread into large cubes to make about 4 cups. Spread the cubes on a baking sheet and set aside. If the bread isn't dry, cut it early and let it sit for part of the day.

2. Peel, halve, and seed the cucumbers. Cut into 1/2-inch thick slices and transfer to a large salad bowl. Add the bell pepper, zucchini, and onion. Slice the tomatoes into eighths and add them with the olives. Stir in the 1/4 teaspoon salt. Set aside 15 minutes.

3. Add the bread to the salad and toss well. Cover with plastic wrap and set aside 10 minutes so the bread absorbs the juices.

4. Whisk the oil, vinegar, and garlic together. Drizzle over the salad and mix well. Toss in the herbs, pepper, and more salt, if needed. Allow the bread to rest several minutes, and then see if it's nicely dampened. If it seems somewhat dry, sprinkle the salad with water, 1 tablespoon at a time, until you've achieved the right texture.

SERVES 6

TIPS: Add 1 cup drained and rinsed chickpeas or pieces of leftover chicken for a heartier dish. Italians know this salad as *panzanella*; it is wonderful made with summer's fresh, juicy tomatoes.

HOT SHRIMP AND CRAB SALAD

Make this a top-hat salad: serve it in Puff Pastry Squares (see recipe right) accompanied by Boston lettuce dressed with vinaigrette.

1 pound medium shrimp, split lengthwise

8 ounces crabmeat, picked over for cartilage

1/2 cup diced red bell pepper

1/4 cup grated onion

1 cup thinly sliced celery

1 cup whole egg mayonnaise

1 teaspoon Worcestershire sauce

1 2-ounce jar pimentos, well drained

1/4 teaspoon salt

1/4 teaspoon black pepper

1/2 cup fine dry unseasoned bread crumbs

3 tablespoons minced fresh parsley leaves

3 tablespoons unsalted butter, melted

Puff Pastry Squares (see recipe right)

1. Preheat the oven to 350°F. Butter a 9 x 13-inch baking dish and set aside.

2. Lightly combine the shrimp, crabmeat, bell pepper, onion, celery, mayonnaise, Worcestershire sauce, pimento, salt, and pepper in a medium bowl. Transfer the mixture to the prepared baking dish.

3. Combine the bread crumbs and parsley. Mix in the butter and sprinkle over the seafood mixture.

4. Bake uncovered 30 minutes. Allow the salad to settle 5 minutes before assembling.

5. Cut the puff pastry in half horizontally. Warm in the oven at 350°F 5 minutes. Place a bottom square on each plate. Ladle the hot salad into the pastry and top with a top square. Serve immediately.

SERVES 8

PUFF PASTRY SQUARES

1 box (2 sheets) frozen puff pastry sheets, defrosted according to package directions

flour for work surface

1. Preheat the oven to 400°F. Line a cookie sheet with aluminum foil.

2. Place one pastry sheet on a lightly floured work surface. Using a ruler as a guide, cut the pastry in half lengthwise down the crease and widthwise across the middle to produce four evenly sized squares. Lift the squares using a spatula and place on the cookie sheet with space between each one. Repeat.

CONTINUED >

3. Bake the squares 10 to 12 minutes or until puffed and golden brown. Allow the squares to cool in the pan on a rack.

MAKES 8 SQUARES

PERFECTION SALAD

This salad is an American archival recipe, created in 1905 by Mrs. Cooke of Pennsylvania for a Knox gelatin contest. She won third prize for her efforts. Prepare it the night before, or at least 4 hours before serving, so it will be thoroughly set.

1 cup water

2 envelopes unflavored gelatin

1/2 cup sugar

1 teaspoon salt

1 1/2 cups boiling water

1/2 cup apple cider vinegar

2 tablespoons lemon juice

2 cups finely shredded cabbage

1 1/2 cups minced celery

1 cup shredded carrots

1/4 cup minced green bell pepper

1 4-ounce jar chopped pimentos, drained

1. Lightly oil a 9 x 13-inch glass dish or a 1 1/2-quart or 6-cup mold.

2. Pour the water into a medium saucepan and sprinkle the gelatin over the water. Allow the mixture to soften, about 5 minutes. Turn the heat to low, stir in the sugar and salt, and allow the ingredients to dissolve while stirring constantly. Transfer the mixture to a large bowl and pour in the boiling water, vinegar, and lemon juice. Place the bowl in the refrigerator. Stir occasionally until the mixture thickens and becomes similar to the consistency of unbeaten egg whites, about 1 hour.

3. Fold in the cabbage, celery, carrots, bell pepper, and pimentos until well distributed.

4. Transfer the mixture into the prepared glass dish or mold. Chill until firm, at least 4 hours or overnight. Cut into squares and serve individually on red lettuce leaves or directly from the glass dish. Alternatively, turn the salad onto a platter and surround with lettuce.

SERVES 10 TO 12

OVERNIGHT MASHED POTATOES

One secret of light, fluffy potatoes is to shake the hot cooked potatoes in their hot pot. Note that this dish must be refrigerated overnight before baking.

> bread crumbs
> 8 to 10 (2 1/2 to 3 pounds) medium potatoes, peeled
> 1/2 cup whole milk, warmed
> 6 tablespoons unsalted butter, softened or melted
> 1/2 teaspoon salt
> 1/4 teaspoon black pepper
> 1 cup sour cream
> 2 large eggs, beaten

1. Butter a 2 to 2 1/2-quart soufflé dish or casserole. Dust the dish with the bread crumbs and set aside.

2. Cook the potatoes in boiling salted water in a covered saucepan 20 to 30 minutes or until the potatoes drop off a knife inserted into several of them.

3. Drain the potatoes in a colander. Return the potatoes to the saucepan. Over the lowest heat, shake vigorously to dry the potatoes. Remove from heat.

4. Mash the potatoes using a handheld potato masher. Add the milk, butter, salt, and pepper. Mash until they are smooth and lumpy, or according to your preference.

5. Fold in the sour cream. Add the eggs and combine well using a wooden spoon. The potatoes should be neither loose nor stiff, but just the same consistency as if you were ready to serve them.

6. Transfer the mixture to the prepared soufflé dish. Cover with plastic wrap and refrigerate overnight.

7. Preheat the oven to 350°F. Bake 50 to 60 minutes or until the potatoes are puffed and golden brown on top. Serve immediately.

SERVES 6 TO 8

ANTIPASTO SALAD

When friends stopped in unexpectedly and were invited to stay for dinner or when my parents entertained, I was amazed how quickly they created an antipasto. They relied on a pantry well stocked with cured black olives, salami, cheeses, caponata, tuna, capers, hard-cooked eggs, anchovies, and beans. Thick-crusted Italian bread was a staple, and so were jars of roasted red peppers and myriad kinds of olive oil. Fresh garlic wasn't used because taste buds might retain the flavor, which would ruin dinner. With a huge glass bowl of vinaigrette-dressed romaine lettuce salad as the centerpiece, the antipasto tray became an Italian salad bar.

White Beans

2 16-ounce cans white or cannellini beans, drained, rinsed, shaken, and patted dry
1/4 teaspoon salt
1/4 teaspoon black pepper
2 slices red onion, soaked in ice water, drained, patted dry, and minced
2 sprigs parsley leaves, rinsed, dried, and chopped
1/3 to 1/2 cup extra-virgin or virgin olive oil

1. Place the beans in a serving bowl and toss with the salt and pepper.

2. Add the onion, parsley, and oil. Toss the ingredients together using two spoons to combine.

3. Cover and leave at room temperature until needed.

4. Place the bowl in the center of a large tray or platter. This mixture can be put on lettuce, spread on Italian bread, or eaten from a small plate.

Serves 6

TIP: Combine beans with a 1-pound can of Roman or light red kidney beans for a pretty two-color bowlful, or use garbanzo beans only and prepare as above.

Vegetables

Cooked fresh green beans, asparagus, and carrots dressed with olive oil, herbs, and salt and pepper are popular antipasto ingredients. Jarred tiny pickled beets, marinated mushrooms and artichoke hearts, and canned caponata are always present; in season add fresh ruby red tomatoes in slices or quarters dressed with a sprinkle of olive oil and fresh basil.

Salami

Peel the rind using a sharp paring knife or vegetable peeler. Cut paper-thin slices from the roll and cut in half.

Prosciutto

Purchase thin slices of prosciutto at an Italian deli. Cut the long pieces in half horizontally and roll.

Roasted Red Peppers

These come packed in large jars. Drain the peppers and pat dry. Slice into thin strips. Place in a bowl and season with a little olive oil, pepper, and capers.

Tuna

Purchase Italian tuna packed in olive oil for authentic flavor. Drain, place in a serving dish, flake, and sprinkle with a little pepper.

Hard-cooked Eggs

Cut into quarters and arrange among the rows of meats, cheeses, and vegetables.

Green and Black Olives

Olives come packed in brine; rinse before using. Sprinkle olives and capers over the antipasto ingredients and have more in bowls nearby. Olives also lend themselves to being dressed: Mix rinsed olives with a little orange and lemon zest, a few red pepper flakes, and a light shower of olive oil. Have dishes available for discarding the pits.

Capers

These little buds from Mediterranean bushes come packed in brine or salt. Rinse before using.

Italian Cheese Plate

Select three to five cheeses depending on how many guests are being served and whether it is the centerpiece of the antipasto. The cheeses should go well together and reflect your tastes. The following are only a few of the Italian cheeses available.

Mozzarella

Cut this soft mild cheese into cubes. If you bought a mozzarella braid, place it on a board with a knife so guests can cut it. Mozzarella is delicious plain or dipped into olive oil.

Ricotta

This soft cheese is nice as a savory spread on Italian bread with a drizzle of olive oil and black pepper. As a sweet, drizzle the ricotta with a little honey and serve as a spread with fresh fruit.

Parmegiano-Reggiano and Asiago

Versatile and with a strong personality, these cheeses come in wedges and are great for grating and eating out of your hand on their own or with Italian bread or water crackers. Shave curls from the wedges and leave on the board for tasting, in the salad, or for eating with fruit. Present small clusters of white and red grapes on a plate, as well as unpeeled apple slices brushed with orange or lemon juice, and other cut fruits to accompany the Italian cheeses.

Continued >

Provolone

Provolone is a semi-hard, strongly flavored cheese that usually comes in a rope-tied ball. Remove the rope, cut the ball in half, either horizontally or lengthwise, and serve a wedge at a time on a cheese board accompanied by a hard cheese knife or small cheese cleaver.

Pecorino

With a pale golden color and gentle flavor, this sheep's milk cheese is easy to enjoy with fruit or sprinkled over an antipasto salad.

Presentation:

Place the small-bite items and the white beans in the center of a large platter, tray, or lazy Susan with the other ingredients radiating out in rows from the center to the edges. Present a big salad of mixed lettuces in a separate bowl. Baskets for holding small pieces of plain and toasted Italian bread, small dishes for olive oil, a cruet of vinegar to dress the antipasto, and salt and pepper should be nearby.

FAMILY FAVORITES

This group of versatile casseroles has withstood the test of time, enduring countless variations to earn membership in the category of Family Favorites. Macaroni and Cheese Casserole I and II, Shepherd's Cottage Pie, and Green Bean Casserole are the golden oldies we turn to repeatedly for potlucks. Many nostalgic favorites, such as Virginia Corn Pudding Casserole and Three Onion au Gratin Casserole, hold a meal together. Chicken Wild Rice Casserole with its many variations as well as Lasagna and Tuna Noodle Casserole have maintained their preeminent status as the favorites everyone looks forward to on potluck tables across America.

SHEPHERD'S COTTAGE PIE

Brought to America by immigrants from the British Isles, this homespun casserole originated as a way to use leftovers from Sunday dinner. Even today it's a mainstay on pub menus throughout Great Britain. Called Shepherd's Pie when made with lamb and Shepherd's Cottage Pie with beef, this one-dish meal easily accommodates a crowd. The combination of flour and oil cooked to make a roux adds depth of flavor to the finished pie. Note that the pie is refrigerated at least 1 hour before baking.

2 beef bouillon cubes

2/3 cup boiling water

4 tablespoons vegetable oil

3 tablespoons all-purpose flour

1 medium yellow onion, chopped

1 1/2 pounds lean ground beef, or 3 to 4 cups
    cold cooked beef or lamb, cubed

1 1/2 teaspoons dried marjoram leaves

1 14.5-ounce can stewed tomatoes

2 teaspoons sweet paprika

1 1/2 cups frozen peas and carrots

1/2 cup frozen corn (optional)

1 2.8-ounce can french fried onions

1 10 3/4-ounce can cream of mushroom soup

3 to 4 cups mashed potatoes (1 1/2 to 2 pounds
    potatoes or instant)

2 teaspoons dried chives

1. Butter a 10-inch deep-dish pie plate, 9 x 13-inch baking dish, or 2 1/2-quart au gratin dish and set aside.

2. Combine bouillon cubes in water and set aside.

3. Warm the oil over moderately low heat in a large skillet and add the flour, stirring to blend. Cook until caramel colored. Increase the heat to medium, stir in the onion, add the meat, and cook until the meat is no longer pink, breaking up the larger pieces with the side of a wooden spoon. Stir in the marjoram. Stir in the bouillon, tomatoes, and paprika. Bring to a boil; stir in the vegetables and soup. Cook about 5 minutes or until the mixture bubbles and looks thickened and blended.

4. Put the mixture into the prepared pie plate, smoothing the top. Cover with wax paper and cool in the refrigerator at least 1 hour.

5. Place aluminum foil on the oven rack to catch juices. Preheat the oven to 375°F.

6. Prepare the mashed potatoes and mix in the chives. Spread the potatoes over the meat, swirling with a fork. Bake 30 minutes.

7. Remove the pie from the oven. Distribute the onions on top. Bake 15 to 20 minutes or until the potatoes are lightly browned and the juices are bubbling. Allow the pie to rest 5 minutes before serving.

SERVES 8 TO 10

CHICKEN WILD RICE CASSEROLE I

Everyone I know who has tasted this dish loves it, and for good reason. Its simplicity beguiles, and the ingredients match up perfectly. Try it for potlucks, company, and buffets; it doubles or triples easily.

2 tablespoons unsalted butter

1 small onion, minced

2 cloves garlic, minced

1 green bell pepper, chopped

3 ribs celery, thinly sliced

1 2-ounce jar diced pimentos, drained

1 7-ounce can sliced mushrooms, drained

3 cups cooked chicken or turkey

3 cups chicken broth

1 10 3/4-ounce can cream of chicken soup

1/2 cup sour cream

1/4 cup chopped parsley

1/2 teaspoon dry thyme leaves, rubbed

2 6-ounce packages seasoned long grain and
    wild rice mix, uncooked

1. Preheat the oven to 350°F. Lightly butter a deep 9 x 13-inch baking dish and set aside.

2. Melt the butter in a large skillet over moderate heat. Add the onion, garlic, bell pepper, and celery; sauté until soft.

3. Place the pimentos, mushrooms, chicken, broth, soup, sour cream, parsley, and thyme in a large bowl. Add the sautéed ingredients and mix to combine thoroughly. Fold in the rice mix with its seasoning packets until well distributed.

4. Transfer the mixture to the prepared baking dish, leveling it off with a spatula. Bake covered, 50 minutes. Uncover and bake 15 to 30 minutes or until the liquid has been absorbed. Allow the dish to settle 15 minutes before serving.

SERVES 6 TO 8

CHICKEN WILD RICE CASSEROLE II

This casserole accommodates any number of buffet guests. Fill two or three casseroles instead of putting too much in one because this dish bubbles a lot while it bakes.

    2 6-ounce packages seasoned long grain and wild rice
        mix, uncooked
    8 to 10 cups cooked chicken, cut into bite-size pieces
    salt and black pepper
    2 10 3/4-ounce cans cream of chicken soup
    1 10 3/4-ounce can cream of mushroom soup
    1 16-ounce can whole tomatoes, well drained and crushed
    2/3 cup dry white table wine
    8 ounces button mushrooms, rinsed, spun dry, and sliced
    1 tablespoon thyme leaves
    2 tablespoons chopped fresh parsley

1. Preheat the oven to 325°F. Butter a deep 10 x 15-inch casserole or two 9 x 13-inch casseroles and set aside.

2. Reserve the packets of seasonings and distribute the rice mix over the bottom of the prepared casserole. Place the chicken pieces over the rice and sprinkle with the contents of the reserved seasonings packets.

3. Mix the soups with the tomatoes, wine, mushrooms, thyme, and parsley in a large bowl until thoroughly combined. Pour the mixture evenly over the chicken, tilting the pan to distribute, if necessary. Cover tightly with aluminum foil.

4. Bake 1 1/4 hours. Remove the foil and bake 45 minutes to 1 hour or until the juices bubble and the top is golden brown.

SERVES 12 TO 14

TIPS: Use cooked turkey instead of chicken or combine the two in one dish. In summer, use fresh herbs to add vibrant seasoning.

SHEILAH'S CHICKEN ENCHILADAS

This is Sheilah Kaufman's favorite dish. She makes it months ahead and freezes it so it's always at the ready for a potluck. She likes extra sauce so she doubles the sauce ingredients.

    2 whole chicken breasts, halved
    1 teaspoon salt
    2 tablespoons unsalted butter
    1 medium onion, chopped
    1 to 2 cloves garlic, finely minced
    1 4-ounce can chopped green chiles, well drained

1 16-ounce can whole tomatoes, chopped, with liquid

1 8-ounce can tomato sauce

1 teaspoon sugar

1 teaspoon ground cumin

1/2 teaspoon salt

1/2 teaspoon dried oregano leaves

1/2 teaspoon dried basil leaves

12 corn tortillas

2 cups grated Monterey Jack cheese, divided

3/4 cup sour cream

1. Preheat the oven to 350°F. Lightly oil a 9 x 13-inch baking dish and set aside.

2. Place the chicken in a large saucepan with the salt and enough water to cover. Cook covered over moderately low heat until done. Remove from the heat and drain. When cool cut into strips, discarding skin and bones.

3. Melt the butter in a medium saucepan and sauté the onion and garlic until just beginning to turn golden. Stir in the chiles, tomatoes, tomato sauce, sugar, and seasonings. Reduce the temperature and simmer, covered, 20 minutes. Place some of this sauce in the bottom of the prepared baking dish.

4. Place a few pieces of chicken and some cheese in each tortilla. Roll the tortilla and place it seam side down in the sauce. Continue with all tortillas.

5. Combine the sour cream with the remaining sauce and pour over the tortillas, making sure they are well covered. The dish can be covered and refrigerated or frozen at this point.

6. If refrigerated, uncover and sprinkle the remaining cheese on top. Bake 30 to 40 minutes or until ingredients bubble and the cheese melts. Serve this dish piping hot. Insert a clean table knife into a couple of places and feel the tip to determine if the ingredients are uniformly hot.

SERVES 6

TIP: If you take this dish directly from the freezer to the oven, bake covered 30 minutes, uncover, sprinkle the remaining cheese on top, and bake at least another 30 minutes or until the ingredients bubble and the cheese melts.

VIRGINIA CORN PUDDING CASSEROLE

Corn off the cob reveals its succulent nature in this dish, one of my favorites. Use shoepeg corn — both smaller and sweeter than regular corn — so named because its shape resembles a peg. You can also use frozen or drained canned corn. This casserole goes perfectly with chicken, burgers, pork chops, and roasts.

4 cups fresh yellow corn

3 large eggs, beaten

5 tablespoons unsalted butter, melted and cooled

1 1/2 cups half-and-half or heavy cream

3 tablespoons all-purpose flour

1 tablespoon sugar

1 teaspoon salt

1/4 teaspoon white pepper

dash cayenne

1. Preheat the oven to 350°F. Butter a 2-quart baking dish and set aside.

2. Scrape the kernels off the cob directly into a large bowl, making certain the corn "milk" is draining into the bowl, too. Combine with the eggs, butter, and half-and-half. Combine the flour, sugar, salt, pepper, and cayenne in another bowl. Stir the mixture into the corn mixture and mix well.

3. Transfer the mixture to the prepared baking dish. Bake 1 hour or until a knife inserted in the center comes out clean and the top is golden brown.

SERVES 8

THREE ONION AU GRATIN CASSEROLE

This is such a great casserole to set on a buffet table or to accompany grilled hamburgers. Get ahead of the game by setting this up well before you need it.

3 beef bouillon cubes

1 cup boiling water

8 large yellow onions, peeled, halved, and thinly sliced

2 large sweet onions, such as Walla Walla, OSO Sweet, or Vidalia, peeled, halved, and thinly sliced

2 plump shallots, peeled and minced

1/4 cup dry white wine or white vermouth

1 teaspoon sweet paprika

pinch cayenne

1/4 teaspoon black pepper

4 tablespoons unsalted butter, cut into bits

1 1/2 cups shredded swiss cheese

1/4 cup grated Parmesan cheese

1 tablespoon snipped fresh chives

1. Preheat the oven to 350°F. Butter an oval 3-quart or 9 x 13-inch casserole and set aside.

2. Dissolve the bouillon cubes in the water and set aside.

3. Place all the onions and shallots in the prepared casserole. Add the wine, paprika, cayenne, and black pepper; toss to mix. Level the onions and dot with the butter. Pour 1/4 cup bouillon into the casserole.

4. Bake 30 minutes; check to see if the bouillon needs replenishing, adding 2 tablespoonfuls, if necessary. (This dish does not have a lot of juice; the onions give forth their own juices, too.) Stir the onions, return the casserole to the oven, and bake 30 minutes. The onion tips should be browning and the liquid evaporated.

5. Remove the casserole from the oven. Combine the cheeses with the chives. Sprinkle over the onions. Return the casserole to the oven; increase the temperature to 400°F. Bake 15 minutes or until the cheese melts and the top is golden. Serve piping hot.

SERVES 6 TO 8

MACARONI AND CHEESE CASSEROLE I

Thomas Jefferson served this casserole to Messrs. Lewis and Cutler, who had never tasted anything so delicious. They wrote letters to each other, speculating about the ingredients and how the dish was prepared. They referred to it the same way Jefferson did and, of course, used the spelling of that era: "maccaroni and cheese pudding."

3 tablespoons unsalted butter
3 tablespoons all-purpose flour
1/2 teaspoon salt
1/4 teaspoon ground black pepper
1/4 teaspoon ground dry mustard
2 1/2 cups whole milk
2 cups shredded cheddar cheese
2 cups elbow macaroni

1. Preheat the oven to 350 degrees. Butter a 2 1/2-quart baking dish and set aside. Bring a large pot of salted water to a boil.

2. Melt the butter over low heat in a large, deep skillet. Whisk in the flour, salt, pepper, and mustard. Cook over moderately low heat, stirring constantly until the mixture bubbles and begins to thicken. Remove from the heat and whisk in the milk.

3. Return the skillet to the stove; bring to a boil over moderate heat while stirring constantly. Reduce heat and simmer 4 minutes while whisking. Remove from heat and stir in cheese until it blends with the sauce.

4. Cook macaroni in boiling water until tender, about 7 minutes. Drain and combine with cheese sauce.

5. Transfer the mixture to the prepared baking dish. Bake 25 minutes or until bubbly and golden brown.

Serves 6

TIP: Because my family enjoys "melting pockets of cheese," I push several half-slices of American cheese into the macaroni after it's combined with the sauce. Add 10 to 15 minutes to the baking time if this dish has been refrigerated. Insert a clean table knife into a couple of places and feel the tip to determine if the macaroni is uniformly hot.

MACARONI AND CHEESE CASSEROLE II

This special version of macaroni and cheese is creamy and cheesy. It goes together quickly and can be served both as an accompaniment to meat or as a main course with a green salad.

    2 cups wide or medium egg noodles
    1 tablespoon unsalted butter, softened
    1 1/2 cups small curd cottage cheese
    3/4 cup sour cream
    1 large egg
    2 cups shredded cheddar cheese, divided
    1/2 teaspoon salt
    dash white pepper

1. Preheat the oven to 375°F. Butter a 8 x 10-inch au gratin dish or 10-inch oval or rectangular casserole.

2. Cook the noodles in boiling salted water. Drain, return them to the pot, and combine with the butter until the butter melts.

3. Mix the cottage cheese, sour cream, egg, 1 cup of cheese, salt, and pepper in a blender 30 seconds or until smooth. Pour into the cooked noodles and fold together.

4. Transfer the mixture to the prepared au gratin dish; shake it back and forth to level the ingredients. Sprinkle the remaining 1 cup cheese on top.

5. Bake 40 to 45 minutes or until top is lightly golden.

SERVES 6 TO 8

TIPS: Prepare spiced macaroni and cheese by adding a dash of hot sauce or cayenne to the cottage cheese mixture. Seasonings such as ground cumin give a decided Mexican flavor; a little curry powder is reminiscent of Indian dishes.

GREEN BEAN CASSEROLE

This is a splendid combination dish for holiday dinners and beyond. I use fresh or frozen green beans, and I double the fried onions to pump up the flavor.

cut green beans: 2 9-ounce packages frozen,
    cooked and drained; or 1 1/2 to 2 pounds fresh,
    trimmed, cleaned, cut in 1-inch lengths, cooked,
    and drained; or 2 14.5-ounce cans, drained
3/4 cup milk
1 10 3/4-ounce can cream of mushroom soup
pinch black pepper
1 6-ounce can french fried onions, divided

1. Preheat oven to 350°F. Butter a shallow 2 1/2-quart casserole or a 10-inch oval baking dish and set aside.

2. Combine all the ingredients and 1 cup of the onions in a large bowl. Transfer the mixture to the prepared casserole.

3. Bake uncovered 25 minutes. Distribute the remaining onions over the top. Bake 10 minutes or until beans are hot and bubbly and the onions are golden brown.

SERVES 6 TO 8

TIPS: Use scissors to trim and cut fresh green beans. Sometimes I add 1 teaspoon of soy sauce to the mixture to create a different and more delicious flavor dimension. You can prepare the dish the day before and refrigerate, covered, overnight. Add 10 minutes to the baking time if it is cold when you put it in the oven.

SEAFOOD, CREOLE STYLE

This is a classic American dish from Naw'lins and one of the easiest to cook. Serve with white rice.

2 1/2 pounds medium shrimp, shelled and deveined
2 pounds cod fillets, cut into 2-inch pieces
2 7-ounce cans minced clams, liquid reserved
4 tablespoons vegetable oil or butter
4 tablespoons all-purpose flour
1 large onion, minced
1 green bell pepper, minced
1 cup finely chopped celery
3 cloves garlic, finely minced
1 teaspoon dried thyme leaves, crushed
1/2 teaspoon grated lemon rind
3 14.5-ounce cans stewed tomatoes,
    crushed, with juice
1 8-ounce can tomato sauce
1 cup water

1 bay leaf

1/2 teaspoon salt

1/2 teaspoon hot sauce or more, to taste

1/4 teaspoon black pepper

2 teaspoons fresh lemon juice

1/4 cup minced fresh parsley leaves

4 cups cooked hot white rice

1. Clean and prepare the shrimp and cod. Cover and refrigerate. Drain the liquid from the clams, set both aside.

2. Heat the oil over moderate heat and stir in the flour. Continue stirring until it turns a caramel color. Reduce the heat to low, add the onion, bell pepper, celery, garlic, thyme, and lemon rind. Cook 4 minutes while stirring. Add the tomatoes, tomato sauce, water, bay leaf, and reserved clam liquid. Bring to a boil, reduce the heat, cover, and cook 15 minutes at a simmer. Stir in the salt, hot sauce, and pepper.

3. Add the cod, return to a simmer, cover, and cook 10 to 12 minutes. Add the shrimp and clams; simmer 10 minutes until the shrimp are pink and tender. Stir in the lemon juice and parsley.

4. Mound the rice in the center of a large serving platter. Surround it with the seafood. Sprinkle with more parsley, if desired.

SERVES AT LEAST 8

JOHNNY MARZETTI'S BEEF OMELET CASSEROLE

Each of Johnny's casseroles comes with a story. Whether he made this one to accommodate unexpected guests or to cook for his family really doesn't matter.

4 tablespoons vegetable oil

1 medium onion, chopped

1 pound lean ground chuck or round

1 teaspoon basil leaves

1/2 teaspoon salt

1 10-ounce box frozen chopped spinach, thawed and drained

8 large eggs, beaten

hot sauce, to taste

1/4 cup grated Parmesan cheese

1. Preheat the oven to 350°F.

2. Wrap the handle of a large skillet with aluminum foil so it is heat resistant. Warm the oil in the skillet, add the onion and meat, and cook until the meat is no longer pink, while breaking up the large pieces. Add the basil, salt, and spinach; cook 15 minutes while stirring to combine.

CONTINUED >

3. Season the eggs with a few drops of hot sauce. Pour the eggs over the meat and spinach mixture; shake the skillet a few times to even out the eggs.

4. Place the skillet in the oven and cook 20 minutes or until the omelet is set and beginning to brown. Sprinkle with the cheese. Cut into 6 or 8 wedges and serve hot or at room temperature with toasted Italian bread.

SERVES 6 TO 8

LASAGNA CASSEROLE

This is the recipe for traditional lasagna my family prepared only for holidays and company. My mother considered it a celebration dish and prepared seemingly hundreds of tiny meatballs in a ton of sauce.

Meatballs:
1 1/2 pounds lean ground beef
1/4 pound ground pork
1/4 pound ground veal
2 large eggs, beaten
2 cloves garlic, minced
3 tablespoons minced parsley
1 teaspoon salt
1/4 teaspoon pepper

1/4 to 1/2 cup bread crumbs
1/4 cup grated Parmesan cheese

Sauce:
2 28-ounce cans crushed tomatoes
1 28-ounce can whole tomatoes
1 6-ounce can tomato paste
1/4 cup olive or vegetable oil
2 cloves garlic, sliced
1 tablespoon Italian seasoning
1 teaspoon dried basil leaves
2 teaspoons salt
1/4 teaspoon black pepper

Casserole:
1 pound ricotta
1 1-pound package lasagna noodles, uncooked
1 1-pound ball or block mozzarella cheese, shredded and divided
1 1/2 cups grated Parmesan cheese, divided

1. To make the meatballs, combine the meats in a large bowl. Add the remaining ingredients and combine well. Roll 30 to 40 teaspoon-size meatballs, or larger, if you prefer. Refrigerate.

2. To make the sauce, place the tomatoes and tomato paste in a large Dutch oven or other heavy pot and stir to combine. Bring to a slow boil over moderately low heat. Turn to simmer.

3. Warm the oil in a large skillet, add the garlic, and remove when it turns golden. Add several meatballs and lightly brown them. Remove the meatballs with a slotted spoon and place them in the simmering sauce. Continue browning the meatballs until they are all in the sauce. Alternatively, bake the meatballs 15 to 17 minutes in a 400°F oven on a baking pan with sides, turning them over after 10 minutes. Add to the sauce.

4. Bring the sauce to boiling. Add the Italian seasoning, basil, salt, and pepper. Stir to combine. Reduce the heat to moderate, cover, and simmer 2 hours, stirring occasionally. If the sauce thickens too much, stir in 1/4 cup water.

5. Place the ricotta in a fine-mesh strainer and push it through using a wooden spoon. Add 1/4 to 1/3 cup sauce (without meatballs) to the ricotta to thin it and make it easy to spread. Set aside.

6. Preheat oven to 350°F. Oil the bottom and sides of a 9 x 13-inch casserole. Ladle 1 cup sauce (without meatballs) on the bottom. Place as many lasagna noodles as will fit close together in the sauce. Ladle 1/2 cup sauce with meatballs over the noodles. Drop tablespoonfuls of half the ricotta mixture over the sauce and spread it in an even layer. Top with some mozzarella and 1/4 cup Parmesan cheese. Continue layering, ending with sauce topped with cheeses. Two or three layers of noodles create satisfying lasagna.

7. Place a loose tent of foil over the lasagna. Bake 45 minutes. Remove the foil and bake 10 to 15 minutes or until the sauce bubbles and the cheese is melted and golden brown.

8. Allow lasagna to settle 15 minutes before cutting.

SERVES 10 TO 12

TIPS: Straining the ricotta, which makes a lighter lasagna without a thick ricotta layer, is my great-grandmother's technique. If you prefer meat sauce without meatballs, mix all the meatball ingredients and brown the mixture in a skillet. Then add to the sauce. I prepared this style of lasagna with meat sauce (no meatballs) with another parent for ten years while my children were in school. It was the major fundraiser for the Student Foreign Exchange Program, which was hugely successful and enriched the coffers every year. We also took orders for trays of take-home lasagna.

They'll Sing for this Supper!

TUNA NOODLE CASSEROLE I

This casserole heads the list of all family favorites.

 3 tablespoons unsalted butter
 1 cup thinly sliced celery
 1/2 cup chopped green pepper (optional)
 1/2 cup chopped onion
 2 10 3/4-ounce cans cream of mushroom or celery soup
 1 cup milk
 1 2-ounce jar chopped pimentos, drained
 2 cups medium egg noodles, cooked and drained
 2 7-ounce cans tuna, well drained
 3/4 cup cracker crumbs
 3 tablespoons butter, melted
 1/2 teaspoon ground paprika

1. Preheat the oven to 350°F. Butter a shallow 2-quart casserole and set aside.

2. Melt butter in a medium saucepan and sauté the celery, green pepper, if using, and onion until softened. Stir in soup and milk; cook until smooth. Remove from the heat and fold in the pimentos. Mix in the noodles and fold in the tuna, breaking up large pieces with the side of a wooden spoon.

3. Transfer the mixture to the prepared casserole.

4. Mix the cracker crumbs with the melted butter and paprika; sprinkle over the top. Bake 30 minutes or until bubbly and the crumbs are golden brown.

SERVES 6

TIPS: For a more modern, effortless dish, use the 12-ounce vacuum-packed pouch of tuna; there's no draining required. Or, forgo the noodles and serve over toast points or baked with chow mein noodles as a topping.

TUNA NOODLE CASSEROLE II

Canned peas make all the difference in this casserole. Cooking the macaroni al dente keeps the ingredients balanced.

 1 10 3/4-ounce can cream of mushroom
  or celery soup
 1/2 cup whole milk
 1 9 1/4-ounce can solid-pack tuna, well
  drained and flaked
 1 15-ounce can very early tiny peas, drained (optional)
 1 tablespoon dried minced onions
 3 cups medium or wide egg noodles, cooked
 1 cup lightly crumbled potato chips

1. Preheat oven to 350°F. Butter a 2-quart casserole. Combine the soup and milk in the prepared casserole. Stir in the tuna, peas, if using, onions, and noodles.

2. Bake 25 minutes. Sprinkle the potato chips over the top. Bake 5 or 6 minutes.

SERVES 4

PEANUT BUTTER AND JELLY ROLL-UPS WITH INSPIRATIONS

Watch these disappear! A favorite with kids of all ages, roll-ups do well stacked in a pyramid at potlucks or at home for breakfast, lunch box treats, after school, or dinner. Remove crusts when it's for company, but leave them on for the family.

> 1 Pullman-style loaf fresh soft white bread
> (about 20 or more slices)
> favorite peanut butter
> favorite jelly or preserves

1. Trim the crusts off the bread, if desired. Flatten each slice with a rolling pin.

2. Spread with peanut butter and top with jelly.

3. Roll up, like a jelly roll, from the short end. Place seam side down on a serving platter or in a casserole dish with a cover. Peanut butter and jelly roll-ups do not have to be refrigerated.

SERVES AT LEAST 10

TIP: Use the same technique with a slice of bologna or with ham and cheese. Egg salad on the bread is delicious, and so is egg salad with bologna. For easy spreading, use whipped cream cheese for cream cheese and jelly roll-ups. All of these must be refrigerated. Pullman-style bread is white bread with square slices and without the rounded top. It is ideal for sandwiches such as this, because when the crusts are removed the results produce uniformly square pieces of bread that are easy to flatten and roll.

CRISPY PEANUT BUTTER BUCKEYES

Bring these family-favorite confections to a potluck and they'll disappear in two blinks of an eye.

1/2 cup (1 stick) unsalted butter or regular
    margarine, softened
1 1-pound box confectioners' sugar
3 1/2 cups crisped rice cereal
1 28-ounce jar crunchy peanut butter
1 6-ounce bag semisweet chocolate morsels
1/3 stick paraffin, chopped into small pieces
styrofoam or empty egg cartons, turned upside down

1. Line a 10 x 15-inch baking pan with wax paper.

2. Mix the butter and sugar together with a handheld mixer, even though it will come out a little lumpy. Add the cereal and peanut butter and mix with your hands to combine. Roll into 2-inch balls and place them on the prepared baking pan.

3. Melt the chocolate and paraffin together in a double boiler, stirring for smoothness.

4. Spear each ball with a toothpick. Dip half the ball into the chocolate mixture.

5. Stick the toothpicks into the Styrofoam until the chocolate dries and is no longer sticky.

6. Store in an airtight container with wax paper between each layer.

Makes about 80

TIPS: A double boiler consists of two pots that fit into each other. The larger bottom pot contains about 2-inches of boiling or simmering water; the top pot has the food or, in this case, chocolate. Melt the chocolate, uncovered, over simmering water, so it doesn't become grainy, which it does when exposed to high temperatures. If you don't have a double boiler, it's easy to put one together by fitting a heat-proof bowl to sit over (not in) simmering water in a pot. The chocolate should not be exposed to steam or liquid because it will "seize" — that is, become grainy and thus useless.

DESSERTS AND SWEET TREATS

Delightful sweets are memorable conclusions to meals. These desserts will carry you through seasonal potluck events, brunches, lunches, and dinners with style and ease. For a big event, the Carrot Wedding Cake takes center stage. Ken Haedrich's Sour Cream Streusel Coffeecake holds a tender crumb, boasts first-class flavor, and has good keeping qualities. Everyone enjoys a handheld sweet: Chocolate Cupcakes, Blondies and Brunettes, and PTA Brownies do the trick. Apple Butter Pumpkin Crumb Pie, Virginia Apple Cobbler, and Rhubarb Strawberry Crumble make the most of luscious seasonal ingredients. Don't forget about Chocolate Wacky Cake and Coconut-topped Extra-Special Four-Layer Dump Cake. These come together in minutes with everyday ingredients — and they're out of this world!

DEE MIRIELLO'S QUICK APPLE PUFFS

Dee prepared these apple puffs for her 2005 Super Bowl party for the Washington & Lee University football team (husband Frank is the coach).

3 large Granny Smith apples, peeled and cored
1 cup water
1 cup sugar
1 cup (2 sticks) unsalted butter
1 10-count can buttermilk biscuits
cinnamon, to taste

1. Preheat the oven to 350°F. Lightly butter a 9 x 13-inch baking dish and set aside.

2. Cut the apples into 20 pieces and set aside.

3. Place the water, sugar, and butter in a saucepan over moderately low heat. Melt the butter and dissolve the sugar.

4. Flatten the biscuits and cut each down the middle into two half-moon pieces. Wrap a biscuit piece around each apple slice. Pinch the edges to seal. Place seam side down in the prepared baking dish. Continue with all the apples and biscuit pieces. Pour the sugar mixture over the apples and sprinkle with cinnamon.

5. Bake 35 minutes or until golden brown. Remove from the oven and spoon the hot liquid in the dish generously over the apples. Serve warm with vanilla ice cream.

SERVES 10

CARROT WEDDING CAKE

Most folks really like a basic carrot cake with cream cheese frosting as their centerpiece wedding cake. This cake is an enjoyable treat any day and for any occasion.

Cake:
2 cups self-rising flour
2 cups all-purpose flour
1 teaspoon baking powder
1/2 teaspoon baking soda
1 tablespoon ground cinnamon
3 cups grated carrots

1 cup currants or soft golden raisins

2 3/4 cups vegetable oil

2 3/4 cups sugar

1 tablespoon vanilla extract

1 8-ounce can crushed pineapple, well drained

5 large eggs, well beaten

Creamy Cream Cheese Frosting (see recipe right)

1 cup freshly grated coconut or packaged coconut flakes

1. Preheat the oven to 350°F. Rub shortening over one 10-inch, one 8-inch, and one 6-inch layer cake pan, dust each with flour, tap out the excess, and set aside.

2. Sift together the flours , baking powder, baking soda, and cinnamon on another piece of wax paper; set aside.

3. Grate the carrots onto wax paper, mix with the currants, and set aside.

4. Beat the oil, sugar, vanilla, and pineapple in the large bowl of a mixer until creamy. Stream in the eggs and beat until well combined. Pour in the flour mixture; add the carrot mixture. Mix on low speed, scraping often, until thoroughly combined. Transfer the mixture to the baking pans.

5. Bake cakes 35 minutes or until a tester inserted in several places comes out clean. Cool the cakes in the pans on a cake rack 15 minutes before turning out of the pans. Cool completely before frosting.

6. Divide each cake in half to make 2 layers. Spread the frosting over the cooled cakes. Sprinkle only the sides with coconut. Cool the cake in the refrigerator 2 hours to allow the icing to set before draping a tent of foil or plastic wrap over it and returning to the refrigerator. (This cake maintains its freshness up to 3 days under refrigeration.) Allow the cake to sit at room temperature 1 hour before cutting.

SERVES AT LEAST 16

CREAMY CREAM CHEESE FROSTING

2 8-ounce packages cream cheese, softened

1 8-ounce tub whipped cream cheese

3/4 cup (1 1/2 sticks) unsalted butter, softened

1 teaspoon vanilla extract

1 1-pound box (or more) confectioners' sugar, sifted

heavy cream

Beat the cream cheeses, butter, and vanilla in the large bowl of a mixer until well combined. Add the confectioners' sugar a cupful at a time, beating until well incorporated and the frosting is smooth. Add droplets of cream to thin the frosting or more sugar to thicken it.

MAKES ABOUT 4 CUPS

KEN HAEDRICH'S SOUR CREAM STREUSEL COFFEECAKE

Big, buttery, and packed inside and out with brown sugar streusel, this is a good coffeecake to have on hand. Can't finish it all in one sitting? No problem: Slice and freeze individual pieces for hikes, road trips, and lunches, or spread the joy and give some away to the neighbors.

Topping:

1 1/2 cups pecan halves or walnuts

1/3 cup packed light brown sugar

2 tablespoons all-purpose flour

1 teaspoon ground cinnamon

3 tablespoons cold unsalted butter, cut into several pieces

Cake:

2 3/4 cups all-purpose flour

2 teaspoons baking powder

1/2 teaspoon baking soda

1/2 teaspoon salt

1 cup (2 sticks) unsalted butter, softened

1 3/4 cups sugar

3 large eggs, at room temperature

1 teaspoon grated lemon zest

1 teaspoon vanilla extract

1/2 cup sour cream

1/2 cup milk

Glaze:

1 1/4 cups confectioners' sugar

2 tablespoons milk

1. Preheat the oven to 350°F. Place a rack in the center of the oven. Butter and flour a 9 x 13-inch casserole.

2. To make the topping, place the pecans, brown sugar, flour, and cinnamon in the workbowl of a food processor. Pulse several times to chop the nuts coarsely. Remove the lid and add the butter. Pulse repeatedly until the mixture is finely chopped into gravel-like crumbs. Set aside.

3. To make the cake, sift the flour, baking powder, baking soda, and salt into a medium bowl and set aside. Cream the butter on medium-high speed of an electric mixer, preferably a large stand mixer, gradually adding the sugar. Add the eggs, one at a time, beating well after each addition. Add the zest and vanilla; blend briefly.

4. Blend the sour cream and milk in a 1-cup liquid measure. Blend about 1/3 of this mixture into the creamed ingredients until evenly blended. Blend in about 1/3 of the dry ingredients until evenly blended. Continue adding liquid and dry ingredients alternately by thirds, beating each time until the batter is smooth.

5. Transfer half the batter to the prepared casserole. Sprinkle with half the topping, pressing it lightly into the batter. Spread the remaining batter evenly over the topping. Cover with the remaining topping.

6. Bake about 40 minutes until nicely browned or when a toothpick inserted in several places comes out clean.

7. To make the glaze, whisk the confectioners' sugar with the milk in a small bowl until smooth.

8. Cool the cake thoroughly in the pan on a rack before drizzling on the glaze.

SERVES 12

VIRGINIA APPLE COBBLER

Different kinds of apples, such as a mix of Rome, Jonathan, Cortland, and Golden Delicious, make the best flavor and texture for this cobbler. During baking the batter rises, enfolding the apples and giving the top a cobbled appearance.

1/2 cup (1 stick) unsalted butter
5 to 6 cups peeled, cored, and sliced apples
1 cup sugar or more as needed, divided
1/4 cup water
1 1/2 teaspoons ground cinnamon
1 cup all-purpose flour
1 teaspoon baking powder
pinch salt
3/4 cup milk

1. Preheat the oven to 350°F. Place the butter in a 9 x 13-inch casserole and put in the oven to melt.

2. Mix the apples with 1/2 cup sugar, water, and cinnamon. Set aside.

3. Combine the flour, the remaining 1/2 cup sugar, baking powder, salt, and milk in a medium bowl. Stir to combine.

4. Remove the casserole from the oven. Pour the batter over the melted butter but do not stir. Distribute the apples over the batter.

5. Bake 45 to 60 minutes or until the apples are soft, the top is golden brown, and the juices bubble through it. Serve warm or at room temperature plain, with ice cream, or with whipped cream.

SERVES 6

COCONUT-TOPPED EXTRA-SPECIAL FOUR-LAYER DUMP CAKE

You can bank on this dessert for speed, cleverness, and scrumptiousness.

    1 21-ounce can apple pie filling
    1 21-ounce can cherry pie filling
    1 20-ounce can crushed pineapple, with juice
    1 18 1/2-ounce box yellow cake mix
    1 cup (2 sticks) unsalted butter, melted
    1 8-ounce package shredded or flaked coconut

1. Preheat the oven to 350°F.

2. Place a 9 x 13-inch casserole on the counter. Place the apple pie filling in the bottom of the casserole. Top with the cherry pie filling, then the crushed pineapple. Sprinkle the cake mix evenly over the fruit. Pour the butter over the cake mix. Distribute the coconut over the butter.

3. Bake 1 hour. Allow the cake to settle 10 minutes before serving.

SERVES 12

CHOCOLATE WACKY CAKE

If you've never made this cake, you won't know how light and deliciously chocolate it is. Its ingenious, speedy method of preparation flies in the face of the methods we've learned. Although usually served with a dusting of confectioners' sugar, I've included my favorite frosting recipe.

    1/4 cup unsweetened cocoa
    1 1/2 cups all-purpose flour
    1 cup sugar
    1/2 teaspoon salt
    1 teaspoon baking soda
    1 teaspoon white distilled or apple cider vinegar
    1 teaspoon vanilla extract
    5 tablespoons vegetable oil
    1 cup cold water
    confectioners' sugar or Speedy
        Chocolate Frosting (see page 113)

1. Preheat the oven to 350°F.

2. Sift the cocoa, flour, sugar, salt, and baking soda together into a 9 x 9-inch baking dish. Whisk to combine the ingredients thoroughly and to distribute them evenly in the pan.

3. Make three separate holes in the dry ingredients. Place the vinegar in the first hole, vanilla in the second hole, and oil in the third hole. Pour the water

over the ingredients and whisk together to combine.
Smooth and level the batter.

4. Bake 30 minutes or until a tester inserted in the
center comes out clean. Cool 15 minutes in the dish
on a wire rack.

5. Sift confectioners' sugar over the cake, if using,
or frost with Speedy Chocolate Frosting while the
cake is warm.

SERVES 9 TO 12

SPEEDY CHOCOLATE FROSTING

  2 tablespoons unsalted butter, melted
  1/4 cup unsweetened cocoa
  pinch salt
  1/4 cup whole milk or more as needed
  1 teaspoon vanilla extract
  1 1/2 cups sifted confectioners' sugar

Combine the butter, cocoa, and salt in a small
bowl. Whisk in the milk and vanilla until
smooth. Mix in the confectioners' sugar in
three parts and stir until smooth and shiny.
Add more sugar if mixture is too thin or
additional milk to thin.

MAKES ABOUT 1 1/2 CUPS

BLONDIES AND BRUNETTES

These luscious indulgences are related to each other. Both come from the butterscotch family and their foundation batter is usually identical. Brunettes, however, have semisweet chocolate morsels mixed throughout the batter; Blondies may have nuts, but their appearance is golden. For best results stir, stir, stir.

1 1/2 cups all-purpose flour

1/4 teaspoon baking powder

1/2 teaspoon salt

1 1/2 cups tightly packed light brown sugar

3/4 cup unsalted butter, melted

1 1/2 teaspoons vanilla extract

1/2 teaspoon water

2 large eggs, combined

3/4 cup chopped nuts for Blondies (optional)

3/4 cup semisweet chocolate morsels for Brunettes (optional)

1. Preheat the oven to 350°F. Lightly butter and dust with flour an 8 x 8-inch or 7 x 11-inch baking dish and set aside.

2. Combine the flour, baking powder, and salt; set aside.

3. Stir the brown sugar into the butter in a medium bowl. Add the vanilla, water, and eggs. Stir until smooth and well mixed.

4. Stir in the dry ingredients and mix until no traces of flour remain. If you're making Brunettes, fold in the chocolate morsels. If you're making Blondies, fold in the 3/4 cup chopped nuts, if using. Transfer the mixture to the prepared pan.

5. Bake 40 minutes or until a tester inserted in the center comes out almost clean.

MAKES 16

CHOCOLATE FONDUE WITH MARI'S SHORTBREAD

Fondue sounds exotic, but it's really an uncomplicated dip made easier in a four-cup slow cooker that melts the chocolate perfectly. It also keeps the fondue at the optimum temperature for dunking Mari's Shortbread Cookies, pound cake or angel cake chunks, marshmallows, or fruit such as apple slices, bananas, strawberries, or kiwi slices.

1 tablespoon unsalted butter, softened

2 1/2 cups semisweet chocolate morsels, or 3
   favorite 4-ounce chocolate bars, broken into pieces

5 tablespoons unsalted butter, cut into 4 pieces

3/4 cup half-and-half, heavy cream, or evaporated milk

2 tablespoons Kahlúa or other favorite liqueur

zest of 1 medium navel orange

Mari's Shortbread Cookies (see recipe right)

1. Rub inside of slow cooker with softened butter.

2. Place chocolate morsels (or chocolate bar pieces), butter, half-and-half, liqueur, and 2 teaspoons orange zest in the slow cooker. Stir to combine. Cover, turn the heat to high, and cook 5 minutes. Stir, turn the heat to low, and cook 1 1/2 to 2 hours or until the mixture is smooth and suitable for dunking. Stir frequently during the melting period.

3. Keep warm on low setting for dipping. If the fondue thickens too much, stir in 1/4 cup or more of half-and-half, evaporated milk, or cream.

MAKES ALMOST 1 QUART AND SERVES 10 OR MORE

TIPS: I usually buy a sample-size bottle of Kahlúa, Mandarin orange liqueur, or Chambord, a black-raspberry liqueur, for seasoning fondue. Feel free to use your own favorite chocolate bars in this recipe. My favorites include milk chocolate with orange liqueur or caramel filling.

MARI'S SHORTBREAD COOKIES

Mari Okuda and I became friends during the publishing process of my first cookbook, *Cookies by the Dozen*. Mari keeps me informed of her global travels, and her original Christmas cards are a celebration any time of the year.

4 cups all-purpose flour

dash salt

1 pound unsalted butter, softened

1 cup sugar

confectioners' sugar or vanilla sugar (optional)

1. Preheat the oven to 325°F.

2. Combine the flour with the salt.

3. Cream the butter and sugar until light and fluffy. Gradually beat in the flour, mixing well.

4. Toss the dough onto a lightly floured surface and knead until smooth.

5. Pat dough into a 9 x 13-inch baking pan with sides. Prick shortbread all over with a fork.

CONTINUED >

6. Bake 1 hour. Allow the shortbread to settle in the pan on a wire rack about 10 minutes. Cut into squares while warm. Sprinkle with confectioners' sugar, if using.

SERVES AT LEAST 30

RHUBARB STRAWBERRY CRUMBLE

Homey, crunchy, and sweet, a crumble is the perfect dessert for a potluck party. Rhubarb is classified as a vegetable and comes in three types — ruby red field, pink hothouse, and celery green — all of which can be used singly or in combination for this recipe. Peel stringy rhubarb as you would celery and slice it into about 1/2-inch-thick pieces.

Crumble:
1 1/2 cups all-purpose flour
1 cup tightly packed light brown sugar
1 teaspoon ground cinnamon
1/2 teaspoon ground ginger
1/4 teaspoon salt
1/2 cup (1 stick) cold unsalted butter, cut into 8 pieces

Filling:
3 cups strawberries, rinsed, hulled, and sliced
3 tablespoons seedless strawberry preserves, warmed

3 cups rhubarb, trimmed, sliced 1/2-inch thick
3/4 cup sugar
3 tablespoons cornstarch
2 tablespoons cold unsalted butter, cut into bits

1. Mix the flour, sugar, cinnamon, ginger, and salt in a medium bowl. Cut 1/2 cup butter into the dry ingredients with a pastry blender or two knives until it is crumbly and resembles very small peas. Refrigerate.

2. Preheat the oven to 350°F.

3. Combine the strawberries with the preserves. Mix in the rhubarb. Combine 3/4 cup of sugar with the cornstarch and mix in the rhubarb mixture. Toss the ingredients together until well combined. Place in a 2 1/2-quart or 9 x 13-inch casserole. Dot the top with 2 tablespoons butter bits.

4. Sprinkle refrigerated crumble mixture on top, distributing evenly and patting it down.

5. Bake 50 to 60 minutes or until the juices bubble through the golden brown topping. Serve warm with cream or ice cream.

SERVES 8

CHOCOLATE CUPCAKES WITH ICING

This mix-it-all-together, one-bowl recipe brings back memories of the deep chocolate delights I bought from small family-owned bakeries years ago. Note that frosted cupcakes must air-dry at least 1 hour.

2 1/2 cups all-purpose flour
1/2 cup unsweetened baking cocoa
1 3/4 cups sugar
3/4 teaspoon salt
1 1/2 teaspoons baking powder
1 teaspoon baking soda
2/3 cup vegetable oil
1 1/2 cups buttermilk
2 large eggs, beaten
2 teaspoons vanilla extract
Easy Chocolate Icing (see recipe right)

1. Preheat the oven to 400°F. Line two 12-cup muffin tins with paper liners and set aside.

2. Sift the flour, cocoa, sugar, salt, baking powder, and baking soda into a large bowl. Make a well in the center. Combine the oil with the buttermilk, eggs, and vanilla. Combine with the dry ingredients at low speed using a handheld mixer. Beat 2 minutes on medium-high speed while scraping the bowl. Scrape the batter around the sides and up from the bottom to make certain it is thoroughly mixed. Beat at medium-high speed 1 minute.

3. Transfer mixture to cupcake liners, filling 2/3 full.

4. Bake 23 to 25 minutes or until a tester inserted in a center cupcake comes out clean.

5. Cool cupcakes in pan on a metal rack 10 minutes before removing and cooling them on wire racks.

MAKES 24

EASY CHOCOLATE ICING

2/3 cup unsweetened baking cocoa
pinch salt
3 cups confectioners' sugar, sifted if lumpy
1/2 cup (1 stick) unsalted butter, melted
1/2 cup whole milk
1/2 teaspoon vanilla extract

1. Process cocoa, salt, and confectioners' sugar in the workbowl of a food processor to combine.

2. Pour the butter through the feed tube with the machine running; pour in the milk and vanilla. Process until the mixture is smooth.

3. Smooth a generous tablespoonful of icing on each cooled cupcake. Allow cupcakes to air-dry 1 hour or until the frosting is no longer sticky.

MAKES ABOUT 3 CUPS

GLAZED ORANGE CAKE

A basic plain cake becomes special with its sprightly orange flavor as a seasoning in the batter and in the hot glaze.

3 cups cake flour

2 1/2 teaspoons baking powder

1/2 teaspoon baking soda

1/4 teaspoon salt

1 cup sour cream

1/4 cup plus 1/3 cup orange juice, divided

1 cup (2 sticks) unsalted butter, softened

2 1/2 cups sugar, divided

4 large eggs

1 teaspoon vanilla extract

1 tablespoon orange zest

4 tablespoons unsalted butter

1. Preheat the oven to 350°F. Position the rack in the lower third of the oven. Rub vegetable shortening over a 10-inch tube pan. Dust the pan with flour, tapping out the excess.

2. Combine the flour, baking powder, baking soda, and salt in a medium bowl; set aside.

3. Combine the sour cream and 1/4 cup orange juice in a measuring cup; set aside.

4. Beat 1 cup butter and 2 cups sugar on medium-high speed in a large mixer bowl until creamy and light. Beat in the eggs, one at a time. Add the vanilla and zest. Scrape the bowl well.

5. Add 1/3 of the dry ingredients to the creamed mixture and beat on low speed until thoroughly combined. Add half the sour cream mixture and mix on low speed until thoroughly combined. Repeat, mixing in all the sour cream and ending with the remaining flour.

6. Transfer mixture to the prepared pan. Bake 1 hour and 5 minutes or until a tester inserted in several places comes out clean. Cool the cake in the pan on a wire rack 30 minutes before pouring the glaze over it.

7. To make the glaze, place 4 tablespoons butter, the remaining 1/2 cup sugar, and the remaining 1/3 cup orange juice in a small saucepan. Warm the mixture over moderately high heat until the sugar dissolves. Pour the hot glaze (reheating it if necessary) over the hot cake while making holes in the top with a fork. Allow the cake to cool completely in the pan on a rack before transferring it to a serving plate.

SERVES AT LEAST 12

EVERYBODY'S FAVORITE JEWISH APPLE CAKE

Eileen McGrory, my daughter's mother-in-law, sent me her favorite apple cake recipe to include in this cookbook. It's a large, delicious cake and is sure to please everyone.

4 heaping teaspoons ground cinnamon

3/4 cup plus 2 cups sugar, divided

3 cups all-purpose flour

3 teaspoons baking powder

1 cup vegetable oil

5 large eggs, beaten

1/2 cup orange juice

2 1/2 teaspoons vanilla extract

8 large apples, peeled, cored, and thinly sliced

confectioners' sugar

1. Preheat the oven to 350 °F. Place the rack in the lower third of the oven. Lightly butter and flour a 10-inch tube pan.

2. Combine the cinnamon and 3/4 cup sugar in a small bowl and set aside.

3. Sift the flour, baking powder, and the remaining 2 cups of sugar into a large mixer bowl. Make a well in the center; add the oil, eggs, orange juice, and vanilla to the well. Combine on low speed, scraping the bowl frequently. Increase the speed to medium and continue beating 5 minutes while scraping the bowl occasionally.

4. Pour half the batter into the prepared pan. Layer half the apples over the batter; sprinkle with half the cinnamon mixture. Smooth the remaining batter into the pan, cover with the remaining apples, and top with the remaining cinnamon mixture.

5. Bake 1 1/2 hours or until a tester inserted in several places comes out clean. Cool the cake completely in the pan on a wire rack. Turn onto a serving plate and dust with confectioners' sugar.

SERVES AT LEAST 12

PTA BROWNIES

My children named these PTA Brownies because brownies, including these, were always the biggest hit at PTA potlucks.

   4 squares (4 ounces) unsweetened chocolate, chopped
   1/2 cup (1 stick) unsalted butter
   1 cup tightly packed brown sugar
   2 large eggs
   1 teaspoon vanilla extract
   1 cup all-purpose flour
   1/4 teaspoon baking powder
   1/2 teaspoon salt
   1/3 cup seedless raspberry preserves, warmed
   1/2 cup semisweet chocolate morsels

1. Preheat oven to 350°F. Butter and dust with flour an 8 x 8-inch or 7 x 11-inch baking dish; set aside.

2. Melt the chocolate and butter over moderately low heat in a heavy saucepan, stirring until smooth. Cool in the pan off the heat. Stir in the brown sugar. Combine the eggs and vanilla and blend into the chocolate mixture.

3. Combine the flour, baking powder, and salt; gradually stir into the chocolate mixture.

4. Transfer half the batter into the prepared baking dish. Pour the raspberry preserves over the batter. Spread the remaining batter over the preserves. Sprinkle the chocolate morsels over the batter. Bake 35 to 38 minutes or until a tester inserted in the center comes out with a few crumbs on it and the edges are baked.

5. Cool the brownies in the pan on a wire rack before cutting into squares.

MAKES 16 SQUARES

TIP: When I make brownies for a crowd, I prepare this recipe twice and bake it in two pans for more even results.

RAISIN AND DATE STUFFED BAKED APPLES

Although baked apples make a fine breakfast and brunch dish, they have delightful appeal as a dessert. Raisins and dates bring their own sweetness to the dish, making sugar an ingredient you can adjust up or down to suit your taste. Dress up hot baked apples with Elegant Vanilla Cream Sauce (see recipe page 121).

8 medium baking apples such as Granny Smith or Rome,
   washed and cored

8 large pitted dates

1 cup dark raisins

1 cup water

3/4 cup tightly packed brown sugar

4 to 5 tablespoons unsalted butter

4 tablespoons light or dark corn syrup

1 1/2 rounded teaspoons ground cinnamon

1. Preheat the oven to 375°F.

2. Pare a wide strip of skin down 1/4 from the top of each apple. Core each apple with a paring knife to enlarge the cavity. If an apple wobbles, slice off some of the bottom to level it. Stuff a date into each cavity and fill with raisins. Place the apples in a 9 x 13-inch baking dish.

3. Bring the water, sugar, butter, corn syrup, and cinnamon to a boil in a small saucepan. Stir about 4 minutes while at a gentle boil to dissolve the sugar. Pour the hot syrup over and around the apples. Baste occasionally during baking. Bake 50 minutes or until apples are soft and the pared area is lightly golden.

SERVES 8

TIP: We enjoy baked apples during the cooler months when oranges are in season. I usually add a little fresh orange zest to brighten the sauce.

ELEGANT VANILLA CREAM SAUCE

3 large egg yolks

3 tablespoons sugar

1 cup half-and-half

2 teaspoons vanilla extract

3/4 cup heavy cream or whipping cream

1. Beat the egg yolks and sugar in a saucepan over very low heat or in the top of a double boiler over simmering water. Stir in the half-and-half and cook while stirring until the mixture thickens. Transfer the mixture to a bowl. Stir in the vanilla. Refrigerate, covered, until cool.

2. Beat the cream to soft peaks. Fold into the custard. Cover and refrigerate until needed.

3. Spoon a little sauce in the center of a large flat salad dish or dinner plate. Place the baked apple in the center of the sauce. Spoon a little sauce over the apple. Serve immediately.

MAKES ABOUT 2 CUPS

APPLE BUTTER PUMPKIN CRUMB PIE

This recipe comes from the archival files of a Pennsylvania-Dutch cook. Although all apple butters are delicious, they're not equal when used as pie fillings, so pumpkin purée unites with apple butter to make the right consistency. Topped with buttery crumbs, this pie has more pizzazz than plain ol' pumpkin pie, and it takes its rightful place as the head of Thanksgiving desserts.

Topping:
1 cup all-purpose flour
1 cup light brown sugar
1 teaspoon ground cinnamon
1/4 teaspoon ground ginger
pinch salt
1/2 cup (1 stick) unsalted butter, cut into 8 pieces

Filling:
1 cup apple butter
1 cup pumpkin purée (unseasoned solid pack)
3/4 cup sugar
1 tablespoon all-purpose flour
1 teaspoon ground cinnamon
2 large eggs, beaten
1 teaspoon vanilla extract
1 cup heavy cream
pastry for a single-crust 10-inch pie
zest of 1 medium navel orange

1. Preheat the oven to 425°F. Position the rack in the lower third of the oven.

2. Combine the flour, sugar, cinnamon, ginger, and salt together in a large bowl. Cut in the butter using a pastry blender or two knives until the mixture is crumbly and resembles very small peas. Place the topping in a smaller bowl, cover, and refrigerate.

3. Combine the apple butter, pumpkin, sugar, flour, and cinnamon in the large bowl. Beat in the eggs and vanilla using a handheld mixer or whisk. Add the cream and 2 teaspoons orange zest and beat to mix thoroughly. Fold in 1 cup of the refrigerated topping mixture.

4. Line a 10-inch pie plate with the pastry, flute the edges, and prick over the bottom and sides with a fork.

5. Transfer the filling to the piecrust. Pack the top with the remaining topping. Bake 10 minutes. Reduce the temperature to 350°F and bake 50 to 60 minutes or until the topping is golden brown and a knife inserted in the center comes out clean.

6. Cool the pie completely before serving.

SERVES 8 TO 10

MENU PLANNING

When I design menus for special potlucks, I find that it's always easier to have suggestions. The following twelve events with recommended potluck dishes will make your planning effortless. Decide on the dishes best suited for the occasion, invite your guests and assign dishes, make your shopping list, prepare your meal, and look forward to a smashing event.

For picnics and tailgate parties, keep hot foods hot and cold foods cold. Hot foods retain their heat in coolers lined with newspapers. When my parents went on picnics, they wrapped piping hot lasagna in newspapers and packed it into newspaper-lined coolers. It stayed hot and transported well. Cold foods stay chilled in coolers loaded with inexpensive blue-ice packs sold in supermarkets. Before using, freeze the packs; they'll stay frozen for hours. Soups and chilis do best in Thermos-type containers: to serve, pour into cups or mugs. Provide crackers, wedges of cheese, and a few garnishes suitable for the meal and the occasion.

I've attend several potluck tailgate parties where the hosts used portable butane-burner stoves to reheat a main course, such as California Casserole or Marge's Western Bean and Beef Casserole. For dessert, nothing equaled dunking Mari's Shortbread into warm Chocolate Fondue. At one tailgate gathering during halftime at a college football game, the hosts provided beverages and requested guests bring their own box lunch assortment of prepared food items in any size container to feed themselves and one other person. Most potluck concepts work as long as everyone gets the same party-friendly directions.

Let's plan a party!

LISTS ARE IMPORTANT TO THE SUCCESS OF EVERY POTLUCK

• Make a guest list.

• Decide on appetizers, main courses, side dishes, breads, and desserts.

• Make a food assignment when you invite each guest. Appoint noncooks to bring beverages, plates, napkins, utensils, ice, coolers, openers, glasses, and a butane lighter, just in case. Appoint game organizers and entertainers.

• Entrust the job of cleaning up to everyone.

A Meet-the-Candidate Potluck Breakfast Brunch
Sally's Corned Beef Hash Casserole
Duke's Favorite Cheese and Green Chile Casserole
Puffy Cheese Strata with Variations
Turkey Pie with Sweet Potato Biscuits
Ken Haedrich's Sour Cream Streusel Coffeecake
Dalia's Overnight Orange Pull-apart Sweet Rolls

A Neighborhood Potluck Get-Together
Deviled Eggs and Egg Salad Spread
Peanut Butter and Jelly Roll-ups with Inspirations
Pam's Black Bean Chili con Carne
Crispy Oven-fried Chicken
PTA Brownies

New Year's Eve Potluck Celebration
Salmon Pâté
Slow Cooker Chili con Queso
Crabmeat Casserole
Spinach-stuffed Mushroom Casserole
Lasagna Casserole
Dalia's Deep-dish Chicken Pie
Everybody's Favorite Jewish Apple Cake
Chocolate Wacky Cake

Mother's Day Potluck Party
Spinach-stuffed Mushroom Casserole
Captain's Country Chicken
Steak and Mushroom Pie
Green Bean Casserole
Perfection Salad
Coconut-topped Extra-special
    Four-Layer Dump Cake

Father's Day Celebration

Clam Dip in a Bread Casserole
Slow Cooker Pork Roast with Cranberries
   and Red Wine Sauce
Baby Brussels Sprouts with Brown Rice Casserole
Glazed Orange Cake
PTA Brownies

Canasta Club Potluck Lunch

Hot Artichoke and Spinach Dip in a Bread Casserole
Natalie's Chicken with Ham in Wine Sauce
Pam's Lethally Fattening Potato Casserole
Virginia Apple Cobbler or Chocolate Wacky Cake

A Potluck Wedding Celebration

Crabmeat Casserole
Antipasto Salad
Lion's Head
Maria's Moussaka
Judith Fertig's Church Supper Chicken
   Wild Rice Hot Dish
Talk-of-the-Town Potato Casserole
Virginia Corn Pudding Casserole
Perfection Salad
Carrot Wedding Cake

Fourth of July Potluck Party

Party Spinach Balls with Horseradish Curry Dip
Southern Fried Chicken
Jeff & Anna's Slow Cooker Chinese Barbecued Pork
Murphy's Grand Potato Salad
Rhubarb Strawberry Crumble
Chocolate Cupcakes with Icing

Valentine's Day Potluck Soup Party

Slow Cooker Meatballs & Lil' Doggies in Tangy Sauce
Italian Meatball Soup
Slow Cooker Cauliflower Vegetable Soup
Slow Cooker Fish Stew
Tammy and Theresa's Slow Cooker Red Pepper
   and Garlic Tostinis
Chocolate Fondue with Mari's Shortbread
Glazed Orange Cake

Super Bowl Potluck Party

Quick and Easy Layered Mexican Dip
Slow Cooker Chili con Queso
Chicken Wild Rice Casserole I or II
Dee Miriello's Quick Apple Puffs

Potluck Funeral Repast

Mexican Onion Pie
Sausage-filled Cornbread with a Side
   of Sautéed Apples
Puffy Cheese Strata with Variations
CiCi's King Ranch Casserole
Beef and Macaroni Casserole
Carrot and Parmesan Cheese Casserole
Perfection Salad
Chocolate Cupcakes with Icing

A Potluck Picnic at the Concert

A-Cup-A-Cup-A-Cup Dip
Crispy Oven-fried Chicken
Ken Haedrich's Wheat Bread and Tomato Salad
Blondies and Brunettes

INDEX

INDEX

POULTRY ENTRÉES

VEGETABLE SIDE DISHES AND SALADS

INDEX